No More Soldiering for Me

by the same author

REUBEN'S CORNER
FALL OUT THE OFFICERS

No More Soldiering for Me

SPIKE MAYS

EYRE & SPOTTISWOODE
LONDON

First published 1971

Printed in Great Britain
for Eyre & Spottiswoode (Publishers) Ltd
11 New Fetter Lane, EC4
by Ebenezer Baylis & Son Limited
The Trinity Press, Worcester, and London

SBN 413 28330 5

When I get my civvy clothes on
Oh how happy I shall be.
When I get my civvy clothes on –
No more soldiering for me.

Army song, 1914–18

Contents

	PLATES	*page* ix
	ACKNOWLEDGEMENTS	xi
1	When I get my Civvy Clothes on	1
2	Bulford Camp	4
3	The Instrument Room	10
4	Evasive Action	21
5	Sorted Out	33
6	Christmas Casuals	45
7	Deadlock and Wedlock	51
8	Gwlad y Gân (Land of Song)	61
9	Counter Measures	72
10	UPW	79
11	Rise Soldiers, Rise	89
12	Retreat	105
13	Auld Reekie	112
14	Mount and March	127
15	Civvy Street	142
16	Newbattle Abbey College	157
17	Edinburgh University	183

Plates

1 *a* Spike Mays, conference delegate *facing page* 82
b Vera, John and Glyn, 1939 82

2 *a* Sgt Mays, Royal Signals
Exercise Elephant, 1942 83
b Spike and Vera
de-mob suit, 1945 83

3 *a* Bonnett Inn, Bartlow Hamlet 98
b Newbattle Abbey, Dalkeith 98

4 *a* Edwin Muir, 1955 99
b Willa Muir, 1967 99

Acknowledgements

I am grateful to the Warden of Newbattle Abbey Residential Adult College for permission to quote verses and lines by students, first printed in the college magazine, *Sun* (Spring 1953), to which George M. Brown, Gavin Muir (for the late Edwin Muir), and Kenneth A. Wood have added personal permissions. Acknowledgements are also made to Robert Fletcher, James Jarvie, Vjera Starcevic and Tom Wilson, whom I have unfortunately been unable to contact.

Plates 1*a* and 3*a* are reproduced from private snapshots; 1*b* from a photograph by Oxford Studios, Swansea; 2*a* and *b* by David Read Studios; 3*b* by permission of the Warden of Newbattle Abbey; and 4*a* and *b* by permission of Gavin Muir and Chatto and Windus Ltd.

Thanks are due to Beecham Foods for kind permission to include an anecdote concerning a Horlicks advertisement; and to the Post Office, Central Personnel Department, Staff Relations and Discipline Division, for kindly reading a draft of my manuscript.

I would have liked to write more about some of the rules and regulations in my experience of the GPO, but was prohibited by a paper I signed in 1936 on the day of my employment.

SPIKE MAYS

No More Soldiering for Me

ONE

When I get my Civvy Clothes on

There's many a troopship just leaving Bombay,
Bound for the old Blighty shore;
Heavily laden with time-expired men,
Bound for the land they adore....

THE MINUTE Tommy Hinton and I had shaken hands for the first and last time with our C.O. in that diminutive bungalow office of 3rd Cavalry Troop, Indian Divisional Signals, Meerut, in September 1934, we ambled instinctively, but unusually quietly to the wet bar of the Other Ranks' canteen. It was a day of great significance. We had to sort things out, over a pint. Tommy had completed his service engagement of twelve years with the colours and was due for honourable discharge. I had completed three and a half years' service at home, two years in Egypt, and five in India, and was due for repatriation to the United Kingdom. Fateh, the ugly Babu, brought two pints of the vinegarish native brew to our places.

'Stone the bleedin' Khedives!' said Tommy. 'HMT *Dorsetshire* from Bombay in a fortnight! I reckoned they'd keep us on till the arse end of the troopin' season... We're flat broke, mate... Half of Blighty's on the dole... reckon I'll get a job as a fitter?'

'You, a civvy fitter!'

'All right, then. Let's go back to the old man an' sign on for a pontoon (twenty-one years).'

'Not bloody likely,' said I. 'The longer we leave it the worse off we'll be. We're like kids leaving school. What the hell do we know about civvy street? The sooner we get the hang of it the better.'

Tommy looked most concerned. I knew why. In the early 1920s we had both enlisted, to get regular meals and a bit of pocket money. Times had changed. Now fully trained professional soldiers, we were completely unfitted for the hazards of civilian life, and were apprehensive about what might await us in the land of our birth. In the closing months of 1932 the commanding officers of most British regiments serving in India had enjoined their near time-expired soldiers to re-engage. Some had produced press photographs of British dole queues, others stressed the advantages of a comparatively sheltered life in the army – free travel to foreign lands, free and regular meals, clothing and pocket money. All extolled the virtues of their own regiments, and the Empire's need to keep them up to Peacetime Establishment.

We scanned the record of our personal military history in the pages of our AB64s, and took stock. There was little to excite or enthuse the Registrar-General about our aptitude for civilian employment. We were both first-class horsemen and remount riders – trainers of Walers, country-breds and arch-necked Arabs. We both held the Certificate of Army Education, not the greatest of academic achievements, perhaps, but sufficient to prove we could count our beer money in English, Arabic and Urdu. Tommy had graduated as a fitter. After enlisting as a band-boy in the Royal Dragoons, and being the world's worst musician and trumpeter, I became a trooper and regimental signaller and could send and receive messages by semaphore and in the Morse code on every known army instrument employed in visual, line and wireless telegraphy. I could also use a lance and the outmoded cavalry sword, and knew all the tricks about spit and polish. Our prospects as civilians seemed grim. More so for Tommy. He was due to become a civvy the moment his big feet touched the deck of Catterick Camp. I had eighteen months to serve in England.

We became more miserable and apprehensive as the day for leaving dawned. Finally, from the deck of HMT *Dorsetshire*, we said our goodbyes to Kipling's 'Shiny', with regret. We loved India, were loth to leave, but had to go.

Seagulls sounded more plaintive and melancholy than ever before as they mewed and flew unseen in Bombay's mist. As for that Indian band that played 'Auld Lang Syne' as we negotiated the gang-plank of the *Dorsetshire*, it should have been clapped into the clink for creating a non-musical nuisance and increasing our misery.

After a loan from a Lancashire Fusilier we survived the six-week trip to Blighty. With this small stake on the Crown and Anchor board we won sufficient for beer and smokes and enough to repay our benefactor. The sailors aboard said it would be a better trip later on, 'Rough in the Med., smooth in the Bay.' They could not have been more wrong. It was so rough in the Mediterranean that we cast a screw. By the time repairs had been carried out it was exceedingly rough in the Bay.

Our greatest shock came when two scruffy tugs pulled us into Southampton's quay-side. Not a kindly black face was to be seen. All the faces of the natives were white as they squinted through the late November fog. At the RTOs office some desk-bound infantryman asked stupid questions about India's heat, diseases and women, before he handed us our rail warrants. Tommy's was made out to Catterick Camp, Yorkshire. Mine to Bulford Camp, Wiltshire.

For the first time in years we were about to be separated. We raised our glasses to each other in some miserable fog-bound bar. Not a word was spoken. We shook hands. Tommy turned right about and was gone. Southampton seemed to empty, leaving me alone in my native land.

TWO

Bulford Camp

MY HANDS became numbed with cold and my mind depressed the moment I saw those green painted tin shacks standing between avenues of whitewashed stones. In the bus at Salisbury I had been told what to expect by a sunburnt Gunner sergeant who wore medal ribbons of Palestine and the North-West Frontier of India.

'You'd be better off desertin', mate. It's the arsehole of the military universe.'

In my first eleven days the sun did not shine once. Not that I blamed it. There was nothing in Bulford worth shining upon. Most of my time was spent in a relentless searching for heat. The NAAFI canteen had a stove which grew red hot after an hour's stoking, then gave up the ghost and smoked so considerably that eyes smarted and tears fell into ice-cold pints of Simmonds's ale. Odd bits of bread and sticky buns were planted on the stove-top for toasting – during its hour of redness and heat – by hungry recruits about eighteen years old, clad in oil-stained dungarees.

Not a horse was to be seen in the cavalry lines. Stables had been converted into garages. Instead of the old familiar ammoniac odour of honest horse urine, there was the reek of oil, petrol and exhaust fumes. Tanks, armoured cars and motor cycles abounded; wireless trucks, mechanical cable layers and lorries were parked with two lines of dejected motor-cars owned by young lieutenants. Mechanisation was rife. And in the cookhouse was a tinny gadget for punching dimples into rissoles.

Because my papers had not arrived from India, because I could not drive motors, or ride motor-bikes, I was the odd man out, unemployable, except for fatigues. 'Puncher' Fee, a sergeant-major who had served in India, took pity on me, and tried to help. Straight from the mess, he was drunk at the time.

'Mays, gotter job fer you. Nip dahn to my married quarters. You'll find a bit of a front garden. Planted bulbs there six months ago an' the bastards ain't come up. Get dahn on yer knees, grope arahnd a bit to see if they've took root. After that report to the Sergeants' Mess. You'll be excused all parades an' fatigues an' be Mess Orderly, in charge of the billiard room.'

I groped under the soil and found nothing. Later he recalled he had forgotten to plant the bulbs. I stuck to the Mess Orderly post for a couple of weeks – only to keep warm. Most of the heat came from the rectangular flat iron I used to iron the baize cloth of the billiard table. I was virtually a prisoner in that Mess. Senior NCOs spent most of their time there playing skittles and snooker, and I scarcely saw the light of the sunless day. When I asked to go back to fatigues I was promoted as personal servant (batman) to a young lieutenant who had been sent down from Oxford, who regarded me as his personal slave. Our dislike was mutual and intense, but I bore his ill manners with some fortitude until that morning I took in his tea, polished boots, buttons and Sam-Browne belt, after his all-night binge in Salisbury. He had spewed over his army carpet and his personal belongings, and ordered me to clean it up.

Standing stiffly to attention I said, 'Sir, you can go to hell. You brought it up, you bloody-well clean it up!' I slammed the door and left. Later that morning I applied for an interview with my Company Commander and asked him to release me from batmanship on the grounds that I wished to study to become a Foreman of Signals.

'Are you sure there is no other reason?' asked the discerning Major Penny, who I suspected had knowledge of the discourteous lieutenant.

'None that I care to discuss, sir!'

Next day he sent for me. My papers had arrived. He was pleased to note that I was a B1 wireless operator and line telegraphist, and that I was entitled to three weeks' leave on repatriation to the U.K.

'Take leave from tomorrow. On your return I shall be sending you to the GPO, Cardiff, to be trained in teleprinter operating and maintenance. Would you like a shot at it? You will be among the first army personnel to get this training.'

'Sir!'

I spent the three weeks in January 1935 with my parents in Bartlow Hamlet, Ashdon, Essex, which I had left in 1924. They were in good health, but tired easily and spent a lot of time in their armchairs. Motor-cars had come to the village and with my ration allowance I hired Len Martin or Harold Thompson to drive us to see my mother's friends in outlying villages and my father's in old country pubs. My brother Leslie, invalided out of the Grenadiers in Kasr-el-Nil Barracks, Cairo, had returned to marry Bessie Ketteridge, thus making her brother, my old friend Christopher, my brother-in-law. Jack was apprenticed to a carpenter in Saffron Walden, my youngest brother Frank was in his last year at the elementary school, and my sister Poppy was working in London. I missed Grandfather Reuben Ford and his wife Susannah. They had died while I was in India. In their old cottage next to ours lived Mr and Mrs Smith and their boys. I sometimes wished Granny Ford could come back again and give me a flick round the ear with her dish-cloth. The village squire, Major Tansley Luddington, whose boots and knives I had been engaged to clean as a schoolboy, was dead, so was Bidwell the tenant farmer of Place Farm, where I worked until the age of sixteen, before joining the Royal Dragoons. There were many new faces.

I was delighted to meet Christopher, who had married his Agnes, had two sons, and had moved from Mill Cottage to another one opposite Place Farm. Throughout my service overseas I had written to him and he to me. We spent a lot of time together, and he told me how the whole village had turned out for Major Luddington's funeral. The farmhands had decorated the wagon with laurel, and the four Suffolk Punches he loved best had drawn his coffin, on the wagon, to his last resting place at All Saints' Church. I was glad to hear that Punch and Jockey were two of the horses. They were my favourites when I worked on the farm.

Life was going on much the same in that peaceful place. It was a joy to walk the fields, paths, and woodlands that I knew. Often I walked Home Wood alone, deep in thought as I traced with my forefinger the letters I had carved into the tree bark ten years before. I had not been alone when I cut those letters and the hearts and the Cupid's arrows. My leave flew like a swift.

Back in Bulford I was introduced to three signalmen who had also served in India and were going to Cardiff with me; Bill Cole from Surbiton, Squash Bramley from Lancashire, and Ginger Jerome from the Midlands. They had served in India for five years in different Signals units and widely separated garrisons. All were expert telegraphists. Major Penny introduced us, a departure from the military norm, but he was a gentleman.

'You will wear civilian clothes. Civilian billets have been found for you. You will be paid additional clothing and ration allowance,' said Major Penny. And then he made his finest statement. 'You will leave here a week from today.'

When we emerged from his office Squash spoke for us all. 'Thank Christ for that! Ten minutes more in this bloody dump and I'd be in the luny bin!'

I used that week to go off alone to Amesbury and Salisbury, to Stonehenge and Salisbury Cathedral. I was baffled by the former, but as a churchman enchanted with the latter. Its spire towered 451 feet, the tallest in Britain at that time and exactly the same height as the top rock of Cheops, the great pyramid I had climbed at Ghiza. I attended a couple of services and heard the magnificence of that mellow organ. Sometimes I would sit on the grassy slopes of Harnum Hill to look down at the cloisters, and was reminded of my choir singing in All Saints' Church, Ashdon. It was early spring, and I was never alone on Harnum. Soldiers from Tidworth, Bulford, Lark Hill and the Bustard were there in droves, some behind sheltering shrub-growth, some in full view, but all making love to the girls they picked up in the 'monkey parades' of Fisherton Street.

We went in fours to the shops of Salisbury and Andover to get fitted out for our new life; to buy civvy suits (off the peg) and strange things like collars and ties, socks and shoes, studs and cuff-links. It was all very strange, frightening and expensive. When we took peeps in the long dress-mirror we did not know ourselves. It was a remarkable transformation. Our faces had been stained by Indian sunshine to a deep brown, the right colour for khaki-drill, but it seemed not to suit our suits.

'We'll get used to it in time,' said Bill Cole, 'but this bloody stiff collar is strangling me!'

At Cardiff General Station we were met by a short fat sergeant of a Signal Territorial unit from Whitchurch who had received instructions by post to find us civilian digs. He beamed and lilted full throat, 'Llanbleddian Gardens it is, boyo! Lovely there. Plenty of good grub!'

He was right. The food was served to our well polished oak table by pretty seventeen-year-old Gwladys who blushed, stammered in lilts, and fell head-over-heels in love with Ginger Jerome the minute he winked at her as she brought in the lovely leek soup. The house was a home from home. Run by a war widow it was beautifully and comfortably furnished, and with beds soft, inviting and yielding, and no reveille.

'Residential, it is,' said our fat sergeant. 'There's posh for you!'

We arrived on a Friday and did not have to report to the GPO until the Monday. We toured the Castle grounds, Bute Street, and Tiger Bay, and on Sunday I went to matins at Llandaff Cathedral. The singing reminded me of East Anglia's nightingales, and I was much moved when they sang my favourite psalm to the tune of 'Crimond'. Things were bound to turn out right for us on Monday.

THREE

The Instrument Room

OLD HABITS die hard in soldiers. We were up and about early on Monday morning, trying to beat each other to the bathroom and to our various bits of cleaning tackle. We could see our faces in the boned and polished toe-caps of our new civvy shoes, and the creases in our new natty trousers were like sabre edges as we walked together, past Cardiff's magnificent municipal buildings and university, on our way to Westgate Street, the street of the GPO, Cardiff Arms Park, and the prostitutes.

At 0900 hours precisely we were welcomed by Mr Nash, Telegraph Superintendent, and Mr Steve King, Teleprinter Training Officer.

'You will be here for six months,' said Mr Nash. 'We are very pleased to have you, particularly as you are qualified Morse telegraphists and must have "telegraph minds".'

Steve King had little to say, but watched us like a kestrel hawk. 'You will start at nine o'clock, with a break for coffee at eleven, one hour for lunch, and continue until five o'clock. You may use the staff canteen. Come and see the Instrument Room.'

He led us into a large room jam-packed with Creed 3A teleprinters, a sprinkling of middle-aged male telegraphists and, to our great delight, a good measure of very pretty girls, a sight for sore eyes after a monastic life in India. We were introduced to some older ladies, who seemed delighted to see us, but not to the young ones. Squash was a bit put out on that score, but cheered up when Steve King took us to the roof and pointed it out as the best grandstand seat for the international rugger matches at Arms Park. After coffee we were tested in sending and receiving Morse on the P.O. 'donkey sounders'. The lady who tested me sat at a remote point behind a glass screen. About fifty years of age, she had the loveliest face, a charmer in black lace, dainty black mittens and silvery grey hair. She sent me the call sign, which I answered to say that I was ready to receive, and then sent me a somewhat disconcerting series of personal messages.

'Betcher can't read this.' She tapped out 'FUJIAMA'.

I sent it back to her, 'FUJIAMA'.

'Wot's it mean?' tapped she.

'Holy mountain of Japan,' tapped I.

'Wrong,' tapped she.

'What then?' tapped I.

'FLIP U JACK I AM ALL RIGHT.'

She laughed behind her screen, and I knew I had made a friend.

We passed our Morse test and were given books and coffee. Steve King made a useful statement. 'Your Morse is first-class. Take the rest of the day off, you will begin training tomorrow.'

We went to the nearby Angel Hotel and drank to the health of Cardiff and Major Penny. Bulford was forgotten.

Our initiation into the mysteries of touch typing began next morning on Imperial Telegraph typewriters specially designed for telegraph training. We must not look at the keyboard. We could not. Our hands and the keys were hidden by metal shields, under which we groped like the blind to find the right keys. The training was good but extremely monotonous, and we soon found that finger muscles well developed for handling rifles and sabres were useless for typing. We were subjected to exercises designed to make us use the little finger of the left hand.

ASS= ASS= ASS= ASS= ASS= ASS= ASS= ASS=
ASD= ASD= ASD= ASD= ASD= ASD= ASD= ASD=

After plugging away at these each day for a week or more we progressed to figures, long words and training sentences.

1=2=3=4=5=6=7=8=9=0=1=2=3=4=5=6=7=8=9=0=
ASSASSINATION= ASSASSINATION= ASSASSINATION=
NOW= IS= THE= TIME= FOR= ALL= GOOD= MEN= TO= COME=
TO= THE= AID= OF= THE= PARTY=
THE= QUICK= BROWN= FOX= JUMPS= OVER= THE=
LAZY= DOG=

'Rhythm, lads. Rhythm! Time and rhythm are all important. Keep time with me. Together, now. One, two, three, four!' Steve King kept us at it for hours at a stretch, beating time with his pencil like Henry Wood at the Proms. Behind us, working like greased lightning on pool circuits of teleprinters which covered the whole of Britain, were the experts. We felt like incompetent mokes stabled with Arab steeds. One day Squash lost control . . .

'Bloody wars!' he shouted at parade-ground level. 'If we keep this up I'll be in the bloody nut-house!'

'Mr Bramley . . . your language!' said the shocked Steve King. 'Remember there are ladies present.'

This had not escaped detection. They were a lovely bunch. Long sex-starved on India's burning plains, we had given them the once-over and remarked that we could be far better employed going to their aid than in typing long sentences about going to the aid of some unspecified party. Although we were acceptable to the older ladies who seemed to have a kind of maternal affection for us, it was not the type of adoration we desired. The young and pretty ones would not take us at any price. Not even when we bribed boy messengers to carry them notes asking for dates. The fact was we were not good enough, not high enough in the social scale. One had the gall to tell us so, and upset us for days, 'You are only *ordinary* soldiers. If you were *officers* it would be different.'

Young Kitty suggested we might be able to find girls of as lowly status as ours in the dance halls of Bute Street and Tiger Bay, and that did not cheer us a lot. But in that day and age civil servants of all grades commanded respect. Their wages were not much to write home about, but in a period of depression they were assured of permanent employment – unless they committed murder, or even a minor offence. For Post Office jobs there were lists of applicants almost as long as Cardiff's dole queues. Common soldiers stood no chance with the daughters of the permanently employed. But we put on our thinking caps. Ginger reckoned that Kitty was right. We might find romance in the dancing dives. And then we made a startling discovery. Not one of us could dance.

'Right, lads,' said Squash. 'We'll take bloody dancing lessons.'

We agreed, then sallied forth to Queen Street to buy flashy ties, patent leather dancing pumps and black silk socks with white clocks down the fetlocks. Next morning we passed a note to the messenger boys who extracted telegrams from the pneumatic tubes as they were pumped in from the sub offices. 'Where can we get dancing lessons?'

They showed our note to the girls, the last thing we wanted. After giggling considerably they wrote down an address, followed by 'Fridays only'.

On Friday evening we paid particular attention to our *toilette*, smarmed back our manes with Californian Poppy solid brilliantine, and moved off smartly down Newport Road.

'This must be it,' said Bill, comparing the door number with the address on the paper. We listened intently. Not a note of dance band music could be heard. Nary a girlish giggle. Just scuffles and thuds. At Bill's knock the door was opened by a sturdy man who looked not in the least like Victor Silvester. This one wore a thick white cable-stitch sweater garnished with bloodstains, one cauliflower ear and an expression of acute annoyance.

'Dancing lessons?' queried Bill, looking a bit sheepish.

'Dancin' lessons, boyo! Takin' the micky, is it? Piss off!'

We discovered that Jack Peterson trained there for the thick-ear profession. There was merriment in the Instrument Room the following Monday when one angelic messenger boy asked if we had learned to dance. There was also one thick ear, expertly delivered by Squash. But from then on the whole of the staff took us to their hearts.

For a week we continued to go out in our foursome, and then realised that by sticking so tightly together we were losing opportunities to discover how civilians ticked. We decided to split up. Bill and Ginger went to different digs in nearby Splott. No one found out where Squash went for quite a time, but it was rumoured that he had found a woman. It was true, his wife had come to look after him.

For a time I stayed on at Llanbleddian Gardens, feeling a bit forlorn until Eileen came into my picture. Her father was one of the GPO top brass; her brother was reading science at Cardiff University. She was a 'check' in the Instrument Room, one of the young ladies who took telegrams to the telegraphists and collected them from the conveyor belt after transmission. We learners were not allowed to speak to these young beauties. To catch their attention we had to give a subdued hiss through our teeth. Talking was discouraged in that place of concentrated industry. But I sent her a note, and regretted it. She picked it up, read it, elevated her pretty nose, threw my note into the waste bin, gave me a withering look which seemed to convey that she wanted no military maggots on her romantic hook, and stalked off. I made more mistakes in typing that day then ever before or since. Her discourtesy shattered my capacity for concentration. But I waited behind the staff exit door that night until she tripped down the stairs, and followed her on foot and by bus to her home in Monthermer Road. I felt like a leper walking in the shadow of a Brahmin priestess. So I wrote to her home address, apologising for being interested in one so beautiful in appearance, but so ugly in behaviour. For a day or two we exchanged glances charged with hate across the crowded, clattering room.

Then I fell a bit under the weather with a touch of residual malaria, and could not go to the GPO. Ginger told all and sundry I was hovering on the verge of the grave with two diseases, malaria and unrequited love. Flowers came, books came, and one evening Eileen came. My landlady ushered her in to the room where I sat shivering with ague. She had brought me a book – and the loveliest of voices.

'There's pity for you. Are you better?'

Her eyes were like smouldering sloes, so full of concern. They took me back to the meadowlands, to Home Wood, to springtime and harvest, and to the initials I carved when I was sixteen.

'I do like you, but it would be the talk of the office. Come to church, St Teilo's. I go every Sunday . . . back row!'

Never before has an ex-Indian soldier been so quickly cured of malaria. Within three days I was back at the key-pounding, to discover that Ginger and Bill had also found girls. At last, we were accepted human beings.

No relapse, visitation, attack or seizure, or even an instant onset of total paralysis would have kept me from St Teilo's Church on the Sunday morning. Without prayer book, hymn book or psalter, I arrived early and seated myself in a pew on the offside of the aisle, about four rows from the pulpit. I was C. of E., and as a choir boy had sung all the hymns, psalms, chants and responses in my village church, and in the fields in all seasons. One look at the hymn board and I knew that I knew each word of each of the five hymns. I did not look round when I heard people entering, but I sensed when Eileen arrived and without looking could have given a six-figure map reference to her precise location. After the service I turned towards the aisle to leave. She was there. In that place where I sensed she was. Our eyes met. A flicker of a smile and a nod of her head. Life surged. I attended church every Sunday. One day Eileen's father spoke to me.

'You don't need books. You seem to know it all. Why not join St Teilo's club? You will meet some nice girls there.'

I thought he must know, but I said nothing and went but once to the club. Eileen gave me a ticket for *Merrie England*. She was in the cast. The singing was like the birdsong, the dawn chorus. We used to meet once or twice a week. We walked and talked in Roath Park. And once I took her to the cinema in Queen Street to see the film, *Let's Fall in Love*. I still hear some of the words . . .

Let's close our eyes, let's make our own paradise,
Little we know of it, still we must try to make a go of it . . .

I made a pretty poor go of it. Sweat poured from me as she sat so close with her hand in mine. This was partly due to recurring malaria, but more because I was distraught. There was so much I wished to say to her, but I was dumb. She was educated, erudite, and her voice was angelic. My vocabulary was limited, inept and had come from fields and farmyards and barrack rooms of garrison towns in England, Egypt and India. When I tried to speak my voice seemed like cattle calls and the croaking of crows. I wrote long outpourings, and then tore them up, so she never got to know, but knew all the time. She went off for the eternity of one week, to her aunt in Aberbargoed. I could not stick the solitude of Llanbleddian Gardens for a whole week. On my way to the Post Office I saw a notice on a window in Sengennydd Road, 'Board and Lodgings'. I took it down and knocked. Wispy, diminutive and kindly looking, Mrs Davies opened the door.

'You don't need this. Can I come tonight?'

At 6.30 p.m. I packed my traps and moved in. Mrs Davies's husband was a railwayman. He seemed glad to see me . . .

'Welcome, boyo! Teemin' with bloody women yere, man!'

Taff was right. There were his three daughters, and a widow and another girl who was reading Domestic Science through a great mane of violent ginger hair. If I wished to learn about women, or become bored stiff with them, I had found the right place. Next morning I went back to Llanbleddian Gardens to pick up odd bits and pieces. There was a letter for me from Aberbargoed. Very short.

'Back soon. Love, Eileen!'

I had no time to be lonely, introspective or to read my books on telegraphy. The time was spent dodging women. Then Teddy Holmes joined us and we males were outnumbered by females two to one. Teddy, who doubled on cello and saxophone and played in a quartet in a restaurant, had the Welshiest Welsh voice in Wales. Tall dark and handsome, he hailed from Ammanford, was addicted to kippers, and lived day and night in evening dress. On the second night after his arrival in Sengennydd Road he took me to his restaurant to listen to the music, and we had a few drinks together, then returned to our digs. Mrs Davies put out his supper. Teddy glared, then bellowed. 'Mrs Davies, bach! I asked for kippahs for suppah and you give me bloatahs!'

We used his kippery comment as a catch-phrase for weeks. Meanwhile, I got to know Mrs Richards, the widow; one whose beauty was exceeded only by her burning curiosity. It had been my intention to remain silent about my military service, since soldiers were held in such low regard, but because I was stained by the sun of Egypt and India I was suspect. The truth emerged through the joint ability of Mrs Davies and Mrs Richards to 'ask' fortunes. They did not 'tell' them, they were extracted by Welsh witchcraft. The minute I finished a cup of tea one or the other would grab my cup, swish round the dregs, inspect the formation of the tea leaves and begin the inquisition.

'You have been over the seas, Mr Mays?'

'Yes. Egypt and India.'

'Infantry?'

'No. Communications.'

'There's lovely. Not married, are you?'

'Not quite.'

'Oh, you have a girl friend?'

'Scores, but I'm looking out for many more.'

'There's wicked for you. Not from Wales, are you?'

'No. East Anglia.'

'Not farmin'?'

'Yes. Ashdon Place Farm. Growing food for you foreigners!'

Davies came to me one night, with a direct question. 'What mob were you in?'

'Royal Dragoons and Royal Signals, why?'

'They knew all along. So did I, boyo. Your regimental number is on your boot brushes.'

To my surprise, Alison of the red mane, the one I thought might ignore me, liked me best. A student from Brynmawr in the Brecknock Beacons, she was full of fun and vitality and would sit next to me at the meal table and rub knees. Her father was an Inspector of Police and used to take her out for long walks and rides through the mountains and valleys of the Rhondda. She told me she loved her native Wales, and taught me bits of Welsh and lent me books. In return I drew charts for her and tidied up her scruffy exercise books.

'You must go to a university one day. Promise, now. It is the only thing worth doing.' She tossed her flaming mane, and I promised.

She was seldom serious. She did not laugh, she gurgled like water cascading over water-worn stones. Sometimes we walked to Llandaff and sat at night on tombstones in the Cathedral grounds. One day I walked her a few miles to the

Wenault, a range of hills rising north of Cardiff, where we had a drink in a wonderful old hostelry, either the Traveller's Friend or the Traveller's Rest. There were soft cushions on sturdy armchairs of oak stained black with age.

'That's better than last time,' said Alison, plumping down.

'Last time?' I queried. 'We haven't been here before.'

'No, silly! I mean the tombstones. Got back with RIP on my bottom!'

Once in a while I went walking with Eileen, but I felt that nothing would come of it. There were others besides me, and they were not common soldiers.

Halfway through training, we had found favour with most of the telegraph staff. They were charitable at heart, but so dedicated and determined to maintain a high standard that they had little time for extra-mural social activities, at least not with us. They never referred to work by that term. It was always 'my duty'.

Five weeks before our course finished we passed the examination and qualified in sending at least ninety telegrams an hour and gumming up an equal number received. Only two letter errors were permitted and one figure error. Accuracy was of paramount importance. A misplaced dot in a stock quotation could cause stocks and shares to soar or plunge and send brokers into delirium. We were warned to watch the wording of texts. Those with ambiguous or embarrassing contents could not be transmitted without the sanction of the Superintendent. Obscenity was out, so too were sacrilegious contents. But when we qualified Mr Nash complimented us and allowed us to sit on 'live circuits' to send and receive to and from the most important stations, 'MF' (Milford Haven) the fishmarket of Wales, and 'TNS', the London Stock Exchange. We were warned against misdemeanours, two examples of which have never failed to cheer me. Apparently, consternation had reigned when a telegram reached the Instrument Room with the following text . . .

UNTO US A CHILD IS BORN SIX FEET LONG AND FOUR FEET WIDE

Enquiry from the office of origin revealed that this was not a record in reproduction. The message originated from the Salvation Army and contained an instruction to a firm of banner makers in Aldersgate and Barbican. 'Unto us a child is born' was the inscription, the remainder the dimensions. The other was a telegram which had been transmitted without question. On the face of it there was not one iota of ambiguity . . .

REPORT DEPTH AND POSITION 0300 HOURS

However, this greeting was addressed to a sub-mariner of the Royal Navy upon the occasion of his wedding and was sent by his fellow sailors.

We much enjoyed working with those talented, intelligent and kindly folk for six short months, and were delighted when Mr Nash called us into his office for the last time.

'You have all attained a high degree of proficiency. You have helped us on live circuits when staffing was difficult, and I am grateful. If you are thinking of careers in the Post Office I can guarantee you established posts here. If you prefer offices nearer your homes I shall be glad to recommend you for any telegraph office in the kingdom.'

We shook hands all round, with some regret. We were still common soldiers, but we had learnt a bit about civvy life.

FOUR

Evasive Action

OUR FOUR pairs of feet had scarcely touched the sods of Bulford Camp when the adjutant sent for us. There was no red carpet leading to his office. Although he was trying his best to look pleased I could see he was putting on a bit of a front.

'We are delighted with your reports from Cardiff. Congratulations! But, er, there is just one thing. You see, we forgot to mention before you went that this course was granted on the distinct understanding that you would all re-engage. You will stay on here as instructors and will be promoted. Forms will be ready for your signatures tomorrow, in the Orderly Room.'

The minute we emerged, and without collusion or mandate, Squash spoke for us all in the old familiar language.

'Stop in this bloody dump instructing! If they give me more stripes than a Bengal tiger and more quids than Tommy Lipton's got tea-leaves, they've had it, mate. It's civvy street for me.'

We did not sign those forms. We were regarded with disdain.

Once in a while, when I could wangle a weekend and could afford the rail fare, I would go to Bartlow Hamlet to spend a few hours with my parents. Some of my fellow farm labourers were still alive and kicking, but because they were poor and married with children to look after they had little time for me. A few turned up on Saturday nights in the

Bonnett, the old pub where we used to meet once a year to celebrate Harvest Home.

My mother looked remarkably well, but my father had twinges in the chest which he put down to indigestion, but it was really heart trouble. One day I received a telegram, COME AT ONCE DAD SERIOUSLY ILL MOTHER. I went quickly from barracks to Brick and Stone Villa at Reuben's Corner, where my mother was born and where I had seen my Aunt Harriet in her coffin. I walked round the back and entered. Mother was sleeping in her armchair with her Bible on her lap. My step startled her into wakefulness . . . 'Ced!' She said it before she opened her eyes. We kissed.

'Thank God you've come. You must talk to him, boy. Won't take a mite of notice of the doctors. His heart's very bad. They towd him to stop smoking that owd pipe, not to walk uphill to the Bonnett, not to drink beer, not to stoop or exert himself. He's not supposed to walk up Church Hill to sing in the choir, but he went twice last Sunday. Talk to him. Put some sense into him!'

I expected to see him in his little cottage bedroom, surrounded by sorrowing relatives, and maybe a brace of parsons to purify his near-departing soul.

'All right,' said I, 'I'll go up and tick him off.'

'He ain't upstairs, boy. Oh no. He's in his garden.'

I crept quietly along the fruit-tree bordered garden path. The garden was as well kept as ever, and there was John Mays, cuffing out a goodish cloud of his Bondman tobacco, stooping and exerting himself considerably as he tugged up a parsnip half as long as the Edgware Road.

'Morning, Mays!' said I.

He straightened, then peered at me over his spectacles through his fading, cataract-clouded eyes.

'Mornin', Ced! What the hell are you doin' here? Have you deserted?'

He had obviously walked the rise to the Bonnett. There was

beer on his breath. I told him Mother and I were concerned about his dicky heart, that she had sent for me because he was so ill, that I had expected to see him abed obeying doctor's orders; not doing all at once all the things they had forbidden him to do.

'It's my heart, boy, not theirs. If I did as they say – set in a chair in carpet slippers – I'd be dead in a week. Let me tell you something else. Years and years ago afore I met your mother I was in Delhi. I had my fortune told by one of them Indian fakirs for two annas. That was cheap. Know what he said? "Soldier, sahib, you will die with boots on." Now, he was a decent sort of chap, and I ain't goin' to let the bugger down.'

Later, he took my arm as we walked very slowly up the hill to our Bonnett Inn. We had to stop now and again.

'Howd hard, let's get me wind. It's indigestion. All that owd curry from Madras and the quack's quinine plays hell with your gut lining!'

We played cribbage, his favourite game. A foursome with Wuddy Smith and Keeper Threadgold, for two quarts of best bitter. He appeared to me the liveliest and healthiest-looking individual of my experience. I was pleased he was fighting it out, but most concerned for him and Mother.

My brothers were now away working, Les in Surrey, and Jack and Frank driving lorries all over the country. Postcards arrived once a week from all corners of the British Isles.

'Where's Poppy (my sister)?' I asked him.

'She's a children's nurse now, in Jerusalem,' said John Mays.

'Jerusalem! I didn't know she'd gone abroad.'

'Not abroad, exactly. The North-West Frontier of London, Golders Green. Looking arter the kids of some Yids. You can tell she ain't home, there's no motor-bikes outside the cottage. When she is them varmints swarm round like bees.'

I discovered that during the time I had spent in Cardiff getting a taste of civvy life, the Army Council had drawn attention to the prevailing civilian mass unemployment, and made arrangements for soldiers within six months of completing their colour service to be discharged prematurely if civilian employment could be guaranteed. For those unable to get guarantees, some vocational training courses had been started at several garrison towns. At Mons Barracks, Aldershot, a course was soon to begin in Electrical Wiring.

Thinking it would be advantageous to have two strings to my bow, and because I wished to get away from Bulford, I applied for the Aldershot course and was accepted. While waiting for it to begin I learned to drive motor-cars, ride motor cycles and operate the first radio telephony wireless set in British military communication history, the famous No. 1 set. This was quite different from operating wireless sets in India which were conveyed on pack-horses and had bright-emitter triode valves that lit up like the signs in Piccadilly Circus.

The No. 1 was compactly padded with sorbo in a two-seater Austin motor-car. Still in the stages of test and trial from the Creed laboratories, it was designed to operate on telegraphy (Morse) and telephony (speech) over hitherto undetermined ranges. To my good fortune a special wireless exercise was started to test its performance. Four sets were employed. Three were sent off to various points within a twelve-mile radius of Stonehenge. I was selected as the operator for the control station, and parked my new motor about eighteen inches from the stony circular shrine of the ancient Druids.

On the last night of the four-day exercise there was a lull in communications. Officers had retired to their sleeping-bags. As signalmen were not allowed the luxury of sleep on such important occasions I had to remain awake and maintain non-existing communications. Because not one dot of a military message was polluting the ether at 0300 hours I idly tuned the receiver to 5 mcs and heard a station transmitting Morse at about twenty-five words per minute. The transmission was automatic and consisted of enciphered groups of five figures. Excellent practice for figure reading!

I had filled the blank backs of several pink message forms before the stream of figures halted. Much to my surprise I heard the call sign of New York Stock Exchange, followed by a series of Vs and the commencing sign for a news item.

MAN MOUNTAIN BATTERED AND BLASTED BY BATTLING BAER

I knew I was on to a good thing as I took down a round by round description of Primo Carnera's humiliating defeat by Max Baer, known for his fooling in the ring as the 'Clown Prince of Boxing'. I knew our Bulford Camp newspaper boy would not deliver this news for at least two days; there were no wireless sets in our tin shacks, and every Bulford soldier was convinced that Baer's block would be knocked off by Italy's Man Mountain. My signal officer was a young, gentlemanly lieutenant. I told him the news in the morning and swore him to secrecy. On our return to camp we each made extremely rewarding bets, he with his fellow officers, I with any soldier sufficiently stupid to put money on Primo Carnera. This proved the most rewarding Morse reading of my experience, and covered my expenses for each day of my two-month course in Electrical Wiring. When asked to give my opinion of the No. 1 set, I lauded it to the skies, stating that Morse could be received loud and clear through great atmospheric interference from places remote. Even from New York.

Aldershot seemed to have deteriorated since I left it as a Royal Dragoon in 1926. In the famous cavalry barracks of Beaumont, Warburg and Willems not a horse was to be seen. Stables had been converted into stinking garages. Where once stood bales of oat straw and sweet-smelling hay were untidy pyramids of oil drums and jerry cans and mounds of oily cotton waste, but not a sign of horse dung. Even the old Veterinary Hospital, once peopled by officers and men of the Royal Army Veterinary Corps, who knew, understood and loved horses, had been converted into a mechanical workshop. And in those tree-lined avenues between Aldershot's barracks, once walked and ridden by my old regiment, was a new breed of soldiers in civvies who appeared ashamed of wearing uniform. It did not seem right to me, particularly in the Cavalry Lines, and I vowed never to return.

My spirits were partly restored the morning I met my civilian instructor. I never got to know his name. We called him Lanky. Not that he was tall, he was even shorter than myself; but he insisted on stressing that he came from the right side of the Pennines, from Lancashire, and that we should keep a sharp look-out when in the presence of Yorkies. Lanky loved living. He had a tremendous sense of humour and his brown eyes glistened like shiny horse-chestnuts. He was deeply concerned that we should gain as much as possible from the course, even though most of us thought our talents lay in other directions. We listened intently to his opening talk (after the brass hats had had their say and departed). He seemed to know about us, even though we had not met before, and swiftly reminded us that we were beginners in the lesson of civilian life and had much to learn about a general attitude to work, the acquisition of technical skill, and a change of outlook after being pampered and sheltered in the army, where, he insisted, most of us had developed scrounging and work-avoidance into a fine art.

'The last folk people want to take on are old soldiers,' said Lanky. 'Most of yer have picked this course because yer think there's not much hard graft puttin' in lightin' an' heatin' points. Yer think all you've got to do is to snip around wi' a pair of side-cuttin' pliers, like virgins cuttin' flowers in convent gardens. But bloody great holes have to be dug to put in brickwork cable ducts; you'll climb roofs, lofts, poles an' trees better'n the apes you resemble; an' by the time you've done you'll have blisters from finger-tips to armpits. Got it? This is where we start, on them benches.'

We signed receipts for metal boxes filled with highly polished tools; drew overalls from the stores, and belts and climbing irons, and were handed pamphlets from the Vocational Guidance Library, drawn up in baffling English by unspecified Industrial Psychologists, and an interesting list of occupational hazards . . .

Muscular strain
Constant walking
Constant standing
Constant sitting
Constant stooping
Acute hearing
Acute vision
Colour discrimination
Dry hands
Handling food

Lefthandedness
Hot working conditions
Cold working conditions
Damp working conditions
Exposed working conditions
Dusty working conditions
Indoor work
Nervous strain
Climbing
Risk of falls

Lanky gave us one more short lecture before we filed out to the canteen. It was to the point.

'This course wouldn't have started but fer me. It's because light is needed. Folks down here didn't know what light were, until we came down from Lancashire to clean yer bloody windows!'

Next day we started off being introduced to tools, various kinds of cable, flexes and switches. Within a week we learned to join cable, use switches, fix fuse-boxes, ceiling roses, plugs and sockets on demonstration boards, of which we each had one. Divers circuits were placed on these boards, with the customary military 'bull'. The insulated covering of the VIR cables (black for negative, red for positive) had to be polished in their colours like the knee-boots of Life Guardsmen, and the brass and steel of switch gear, and even the metal work of the insulated staples, like their helmets and sword hilts. It mattered not that the circuit might not work, and that none could discover why – because it had not been connected to the mains.

But we all enjoyed it and took pride in 'tarting up' our own boards for the many inspections, hoping to get good marks and, eventually, a job in civvy street. Then 'practicality' took a hand in the scheme of things.

At Aldershot lurked many officers of high rank. Mostly chair-borne, married, and living in rent-supplemented or rent-free houses, they were quick to take advantage of our vocational training.

'Why not have your trainees to do the electric repairs to our houses? It will give them the opportunity to tackle real problems . . . far better than listening to lectures and messing about on training benches!'

On the face of it this appeared good sense, but no one mentioned the major advantage – the saving of cost of labour and materials. Soon our trainees were invited to volunteer for 'outside jobs'. Sometimes they earned half a crown between two, for two days' work. More often a thimbleful of tea to wash down one of those socially esteemed sandwiches, too small to fill a dental cavity. At one house on the Farnham-Farnborough Road where almost every room had been re-wired, switched and plugged at the tax-payers' expense, two lads worked for the best part of a week without even a 'thank you'. Only one thing of consequence ever came out of that house free, it was a telephone call, made by the lady of the house.

'Are you the instructah? Good! Those electrician chappies of yours. Could you send them back? Not this afternoon, I'm playing bridge at the Club. Ectually, I would prefer this evening.'

'Wot's up, then?' asked Lanky.

'Well, it's all very tahrsome, and embarrassing. You see, when we pull the toilet chain the lights come on all ovah the house, and we carn't switch them orf. But they all go orf agen when the cistern fills up, and then we carn't switch them on agen. My husband is furious, and says something must be done.'

Nothing was done. The 'electrician chappies', both ex-Instrument Mechanics, flatly refused to go there again. When they enlightened Lanky on their cunning capers with an insulated busch and the crafty wiring of a master switch to the cistern handle – all carefully concealed from human view – he laughed so heartily that he almost blacked out. But we restored him to normal by taking him down to the Ratpit, better known to civilians as the Trafalgar, and putting him outside several large Scotches.

Then I received a card lined in silver and encrusted with cherubs and seraphs, inviting me to my sister Poppy's wedding on 20 November 1935. As they say in Essex, she had 'collared' one Charles Flack, a thriving young butcher from Harlow. Motor cyclists would not clutter up Reuben's Corner any longer.

This turned out to be a wedding and a half. The reception was held in the Conservative Hall – until the booze ran short, then reinforcements were found at the Fox Inn and the Rose and Crown. Poppy was distressed because her friend Vera Jones, an ex-nurse, and a 'foreigner' from Loughor, Glamorgan, missed the Liverpool Street train and the marriage service in All Saints' Church. I was glad not to miss that marriage service. Poppy was dressed in white. Years before when she was due to be confirmed, our parents could not get her a white gown, they were too poor, and Poppy was made a member of the Church at distant Hadstock where none of us was well known, in laced top-boots, grey skirt cut down from Granny Ford's old dress, and a green jumper. It was so good to see her in white.

Vera Jones managed to hire a car at Audley End Junction. She arrived at the Conservative Hall in time for the wedding feast. I sat next to her at table, and have never regretted it. When the party began dancing and singing we slipped out from the hall. I walked her up Radwinter Road, very slowly, and we leaned on five-barred gates and looked at the stars. Then I took her higher up the hill and lured her into the forge of Hill Farm and told her about my childhood sweetheart, Nellie. We were there for quite a long time, two lonely people who needed each other, but very much on the shy side. I plagued her about her Welsh accent and dared her to teach me Welsh, in which she was fluent, and to travel back with me to Liverpool Street.

Three of us had a compartment to ourselves from Audley End to London; my jolly Aunt Sally, who was merry indeed with whisky and gin, Vera from Wales, and me. Vera was tired. She stretched out on the far side of the compartment and was sound asleep in five seconds flat. I covered her with the civvy overcoat I had bought for Cardiff and watched her sleeping, looking at her raven-black hair, and the little crook in her nose. Aunt Sally made a couple of rude noises. She was very fat. Each time she moved more than an eighth of an inch wind escaped from her, followed by a great laugh. She watched me watching Vera and gave me a dig in the ribs.

'Now then, Ced. She's the one fer you. Don't let her go, she's a lady!'

Sally was bound for Islington, Vera for Golders Green and I for Mons Barracks, Aldershot. We parted at Liverpool Street Station. A great slobbering kiss from Aunt Sally; a little peck from Vera, but a look of great importance. She gave me her address.

I did not write to her for nearly twenty-four hours, and then I wrote every day. At weekends when the army released me from its yoke I would go to meet Vera at Sneath Avenue. We went walking in Hyde Park, on Hampstead Heath and other London parklands. Walking was inexpensive, and we could afford it. She was always well dressed, mostly in navy blue and white, and wore hats with little veils that tickled my nose when I tried to get to close quarters. But I was still in the army.

Before I finished the vocational training course something stirred in the Establishments Branch of the GPO. A letter came to my C.O. offering me permanent employment as a Sorting Clerk and Telegraphist at the Post Office, Woking, Surrey. Although the C.O. sent it to me to read and answer I was not able to reply, there being no pens nor ink in the clink. Through giving a sergeant-major the length of my tongue I still had four days of incarceration to serve, and this seemed to put the army back several horse's lengths because my expertise as a telegraphist was required at Woking within twenty-four hours.

'We shall have to let the blighter out,' said the adjutant. 'The Army Council Instruction definitely states that premature discharges *will* be granted if permanent employment is offered.'

Thanks to that ACI I was released from my Aldershot cell. Within twenty-four hours I was on my way to Bulford Camp to pick up various articles of equipment, one week's pay and ration allowance, and a useful piece of paper stating that I had been granted a premature but honourable discharge from His Majesty's Forces, wherein I had served at home and abroad as a professional soldier for eleven years and three hundred days precisely. The final and most generous assessment of my military conduct and character read thus:

Date of Discharge:	11 January 1936
Military Conduct:	Very good
Testimonial:	Honest, sober and trustworthy. A reliable, intelligent and hard-working man. An excellent horseman and soldier with considerable experience in telegraphy – Wireless & Line,

Morse & Teleprinter. Eminently suitable for employment in the General Post Office.

As a civilian, albeit an apprehensive one, I wended my way to Woking.

FIVE

Sorted Out

'DIGS, matey? Let's see now. Oh, yes. There's a nice house down the far end of his road, No. 1. Less than half a mile. Last house on the right. Builder by the name o' Timms. If he carn't take yer, come back to this office an' you can spend the night at my joint at Knaphill.'

This kindly uniformed postman wore the three ribbons of the First World War, 'Pip, Squeak and Wilfrid'. He had emerged from the yard of Woking's sorting office as I was leaving the railway station. The highway from Woking Station seemed strange in terms of its name. It had been christened 'Oriental Road'. I soon found out why. As I trudged along it with my worldly possessions in my brand new cardboard suitcase I looked through a gap in the trees and hedges and, lo and behold, there was a mosque complete with onion-shaped dome, the full quota of minarets and the customary steps to the main entrance. For a moment I thought I was back in Cairo. I looked up, half expecting to see a Muslim priest and hear him call the faithful to prayer. But the wind was blowing hard and large rainspots were doing mischief to my suitcase, and I was quickly brought back to reality.

No. 1 was a sturdy detached house with a good garden. Its door was opened by Mrs Timms, a middle-aged lady who looked starchy and kind at the same time and asked me in to meet her husband. Timms was tall, grey and gaunt, but he had the large hands and the keen eyes of folk who can use tools. I hoped they would accept me.

'From the army?' queried Mrs Timms. Their eyes met, and her brows rose as if I had just escaped from Dartmoor.

'Yes,' said I. 'But I became a civilian yesterday, and I am about to become a civil servant and work in Woking Post Office as a telegraphist.' I flourished my military testimonial and the letter of welcome from the GPO.

'Cup of tea?' asked Mrs Timms. 'Or will you wait for a meal?'

After a meal of good home cooking we talked terms. Although I did not know what my wage would be I settled for thirty shillings per week with full board. Three meals a day and morning tea. Mrs Timms kindly offered to do my laundry. She took me to a bedroom cosy with oak furniture made by Timms. Roses and lilies cascaded from flower baskets adorning the new wallpaper. Two windows looked on to a well-kept garden stocked with pruned fruit trees, flower beds and vegetable plots, and beyond the tall hedge were firs, pines and larches. I thought of my military cell at Mons Barracks, and the tin shacks of Bulford Camp, and felt a strange feeling of freedom, of being at home.

At 0900 hours next morning I reported to Mr Salisbury, a lean, hungry-looking man who carried two watches and an expression of misery. He had multitudinous jobs, Superintendent, Establishments Officer, Writing Duty Overseer and, on occasions, Counter Supervisor at the main Post Office, which was in Woking High Street. His brow was furrowed far beyond his years. He introduced me to his colleagues in the executive part of the sorting office. All wore Surrey public school ties and seemed not overjoyed to meet an ex-soldier.

'There are papers for you to sign,' said Salisbury. There were many, each of them telling me what I must not do, including a copy of the Official Secrets Act and passes of various shades of buff giving permission for me to visit the Head Office and to eat in the staff canteen. It took me an hour to read them all.

At twelve noon I ascended the stairs to the canteen and met colleagues to be. Four had served in the Royal Corps of Signals as wireless operators and telegraphists in India, Ted Hay, Alf (Kipper) Hickmott, Harold Wiley and Joe Shinn. But now they were sorters, clad in dirty khaki smocks whose breast pockets bulged with coloured pencils. Round their necks were loops of string attached to peculiar scissors like miniature secateurs. They all looked very tired and unhappy. Other sorters present had obviously never been in the services. They were grey of face with fatigue and were busy putting pies into or taking them out of a large gas oven. With no time to look or talk to me they wolfed down their meal with both eyes on the wall clock.

'Have you come as a sorter?' asked Kipper Hickmott.

'No. I'm a telegraphist!'

I wondered why they laughed, but soon found out when I spoke to Superintendent Salisbury in the executive office.

'Where are the teleprinters?' I asked, flexing my well-trained fingers in readiness.

'Who told you we were getting a teleprinter?' asked Salisbury. He glared at me as though I had just broken the Official Secrets Act. 'We send all the telegrams by telephone, from Head Office in the High Street. The teleprinter's not coming until next week. This is the sorting office. You start at three o'clock this afternoon, bag opening!'

'I have been trained in teleprinter operating and maintenance,' said I, 'and was accepted for employment as a Sorting Clerk and Telegraphist. If you have no work for me, you have made me obtain a premature discharge from the army on false pretences.'

'No work, indeed. There's plenty here. Don't you fret about that. According to my instructions you're due to start on bag opening at three o'clock this afternoon. Take it or leave it!'

Because I was a stranger in a strange place, with no friends, no money, and now no army, I bag opened. Woking was one of the two forwarding offices for the Surrey and Hampshire mails. Bar one, it was regarded as the worst sweat shop in Post Office history, the exception being Redhill. Sorters slaved at shift work throughout the most anti-social hours of day and night; sometimes with two split attendances, to save the payment of overtime, which covered fourteen to sixteen hours. Bag openers had the dirtiest end of the stick in more ways than one. They were the slaves of the sorters and their *modus operandi* was as follows:

> Seize unopened incoming mail bag by point of balance. Hurl on sorting bench. Remove lead seal and string with scissors and place in wire basket. Grope inside bag for green bill. Grope inside bag for all registered items entered on green bill and check. File green bill on spike. Hand registered items into 'registered cage'. Tip out remaining contents and shove along bench for sorting into road and street walks. Turn bag inside out, fold in four and pile it on mountain of similarly folded bags to immediate rear.

This performance continued at breakneck speed throughout mail reception time (all night) with an Overseer breathing down one's neck, stop-watch in hand to time one's output. This was the most filthy and disgusting job. Mail bags were dragged along many a dirty railway platform before reaching their destinations. Often they contained biological specimens from hospitals and forensic laboratories; portions of persons and animals dead or decaying and samples of animal and human excreta. Although most carefully packed in jars and stoppered bottles sealed in wooden cylinders, the rough treatment by porters and postmen had been known to cause them to break and spill their loathsome contents over business letters, love letters and greeting cards. Sometimes the stench was appalling. I remember poor Tom Smith's refusal to continue one stint. He had been at it some time, but was sufficiently misguided to dip his register-seeking fingers into a particularly ripe specimen of dysentery. His language was as high as the stench, and he stalked off home.

I finished my second day's work at 0300. Dog tired, carrying my cardboard suitcase, I staggered down Oriental Road towards Holmside (No. 1). A beam of light dazzled me, and a voice whose owner I could not see rang out.

'Who are you? What have you got in that bag?'

'Mind your own bloody business,' said I.

'None of your lip. I'm an officer of the law. I want to know why you are strolling about at this time, and what you've got in that bag.'

'Right! I enjoy walking at this time. In the bag I have the Crown jewels and a book instructing policemen to mind their own business.'

'Open it!'

'I refuse. I am a civil servant and have just finished in the sorting office. I have got your number, mate, and a brother who is Commissioner of Police at Scotland Yard.'

He insisted on walking with me to Holmside, more out of curiosity than companionship, and then apologised 'fer bein' a bit hasty-like'. I told Kipper about it on the next shift. 'You can't blame the bloody copper, mate,' said he. 'He was doing his job. Trouble is, until we left the army only three classes of people were allowed to roam about at that hour, postmen, policemen and prostitutes!'

To keep us on our toes we had a minor swarm of supervisory officers of various ranks, shapes, sizes, ages and temperaments, all dedicated and determined that nothing should interfere with the receipt, despatch and delivery of His Majesty's Mail. Just as soldiers are proud of their own regiments, so were the supervisors of their own sorting offices, and, like cavalry

NCOs, some were kind. I had not started to learn sorting, but was witness to differences of approach to the process of 'checking for missorts'. Two of the supervisors would point out, for example, that there were no fewer than five Newports in the British Isles, to say nothing of copy towns in the U.S., New Zealand and Australia. 'If there's no county on the envelope, you put it in the box for the nearest Newport, that's Essex.'

Another regarded a missort as a personal affront to his dignity, and woe betide a sorter who put a Farnborough (Hants) letter into the Kent box. He would redden like a beetroot and splutter like a near-empty soda-water siphon as he denounced the culprit in a high-pitched voice and recorded the misdemeanour on the official check sheet. Always agitated and overheated, he swooped from frame to frame, or sat hawk-eyed on the supervisor's rostrum, a point of vantage from which he could survey the whole floor. Off duty he was kindly and courteous, as were most of them, but the rules and regulations had got into his system.

Old stagers told of tricks they had played on him. Now and again they would steal his jacket from the peg behind his desk and 'give it a ride'. It depended on the distance how long he would remain jacketless. He would calm down for a week after his jacket was returned bearing the label, 'Found in a Woking bag'. From nearby places it would be returned within twenty-four hours, but it took a week for Orcadian sorters to return it from Stromness, via Edinburgh.

When I arrived during my second week, wearing Mother's gift – a natty tie, Paisley-patterned in greens and blues – one swift look and he exploded, 'The king is dead, Mr Mays! Go home and change your tie!'

George V had died on 20 January 1936. I replied with regret, and told him how, some years before on the Great Pyramid, I had received a message by heliograph that His Majesty's health was on the mend, and how I had drunk King

George's health from my water bottle because he was Colonel-in-Chief of my regiment, the Royal Dragoons. I added that I could not afford an extensive wardrobe, and had not a black tie. To my surprise he gave me three shillings and an hour off to buy a tie in Woking High Street. I put on the tie in the shop, thought of my former Colonel-in-Chief, the Great Pyramid, and my friend Jigger Lee who had been there with me, and returned to work.

My supervisor looked, beamed, and softened.

'Give me the three bob when you can afford it.'

We got on famously after that.

I wore that tie for a fortnight, when I went to the lying-in-state, and back in the sorting office. It reminded me of old friends, and the splendour of a former uniform, even though I was clad in the dirty overalls of a bag-opener.

For the king's funeral those of us on night and morning shifts were given the day off to go to Windsor. Those of us on the afternoon shift – and I was one – would have liked to go but could not because we had to start on the night mail despatches at four o'clock and could not have got back from Windsor in time. Our supervisor went, and took with him the key of the sorting office. When he came back in his dark suit – with the key still in his working suit at home – he discovered those of us who should have been working sitting on the grass verge near Oriental Road, playing cards. Fearful that his mails might miss the trains, he asked us to shove him through the small hatch of the lift on the basement floor. With more force than was justifiable we heaved him through. But when he pressed the button the lift jammed and he could not get to the ground floor to open the main door, but remained imprisoned until a cycling messenger retrieved his key from home. We worked like beavers not to let him down. He was deeply moved.

I keep the black tie as a triple souvenir – of his kindness, of my regiment, and my Colonel-in-Chief. It is pinned to the

Dettingen Black, the cloth we wore in Egypt and India behind our badges. The Royals first wore it in honour of 2nd Lieutenant Dunville, posthumously awarded the Victoria Cross in the First World War. It is still worn behind the Eagle of the Royals by our new Household Cavalry regiment, the Blues and Royals.

For two more weeks I opened mail bags from 1500 to 0300 hours, with a two-hour break in the early evening. But on the following Monday I was to receive instruction on the mysteries of sorting His Majesty's mail at 0900. A telephone rang, but there was no one there but me. I picked up the handset, and in my new civil service voice said, 'Good morning. This is the sorting office. Can I help you?'

'Who's speaking?'

'Mays.'

'Come over here right away and have a look at the teleprinter.'

I had to guess it was Head Office. No one told me, but I thought to myself there would be no more bag opening, not even a beginning of sorting.

Half a dozen of the top brass, the executives – whose sole object in life seemed to be issuing adverse reports upon every ex-soldier in Post Office sight – were cluttered round the teleprinter. They looked at me in that superior fashion used by persons of inferiority to cloak ignorance.

'It does not seem to be working, Mr Mays. Have a shot, and see what is wrong.'

I mounted the new green leather swivel chair designed for telegraphists, and felt much at home. I pressed a few keys. Nothing happened. I plugged Vs, and nothing happened, then switched to local, hoping to see my expert typescript on the 3A tape. It remained virginal.

'Now you've done it,' said I to the young lady who had been sent all the way from St Martin's-le-Grand to send the first telegram. 'You have ruined it.'

She blushed, and there were frosty looks all round. I bent down, and pressed the mains switch. The teleprinter surged to life, and I tapped away and established the first teleprinter communication between WLX (Woking) and TS (Central Telegraph Office, London). Bursting to demonstrate my skill, I addressed the top brass.

'Any telegrams to send?'

'Telegrams?' queried the postmaster.

'Telegrams!' snorted the overseer. 'You get back to the sorting office.'

And that was the only occasion I touched a teleprinter in Woking. I felt like writing to Nash at Cardiff, or to the Postmaster-General at the House of Commons, but my pay was important. There was not much left out of my forty-eight shillings per week after I had paid my board and lodging. As usual, I was broke.

Sorting was interesting – if one wanted to turn oneself into a memory man-cum-geographical directory. I was allotted a sorting frame and bench for the Surrey sorting. On the bench the letters poured in from the collecting points, sub-Post Offices and pillar boxes. It was my job to pick them up a handful at a time with my left hand, look at the post town or office of delivery, and whip them into the appropriate box at a speed not less than thirty per minute, the regulation sorting rate. There were forty-eight boxes on the frame, each labelled with a town or district, and it was uncanny to watch the speed and dexterity of the expert sorters. Their eyes were glued to the letters in their left hands, and the letters were placed into their boxes without a glance at the sorting frame. By dint of long practice sorting had become instinctive to them, and the letters were sorted at a speed more than twice that of the regulation rate. I was amazed to find that while sorting at this furious pace, the experts were able to carry on conversations, tell grimy stories and sometimes sing snatches of song.

The method of instruction could not have been simpler.

When in doubt about the correct postal town for some village or hamlet, one asked for guidance from fellow sorters . . .

'Where's Egham?'

'Dirty Marks, mate.'

'Where's Dirty Marks, then?'

'Staines, you bloody fool.'

There was a nickname for almost every postal town, a new language from which I soon got to know the correct circulation for every town, village and hamlet in Surrey and Hampshire. It was all very useful and instructive, an excellent exercise in memory training. I learned the districts served by the TPOs, the Travelling Post Offices, in express trains that thundered through the night from London termini, whose sorting staff swayed on their feet as they sorted to the rhythm of the whirling wheels. I progressed to the London Districts and finally to foreign circulation. We had no maps or atlases, but ask any old sorter a place name anywhere in the world and he will supply the nearest postal town, if not the name of the postman likely to deliver the letter.

Packets and parcels were sorted direct into mail bags suspended by four hooks from a sixty-bag iron frame. Above each bag, painted in white lettering, was the name of the postal town. Wooden trolleys with rubber-tyred wheels would be pushed close to this frame, each piled Everest-high with packets. In about five minutes each trolley would be emptied. Parcels were sorted from large wicker-work skips with clanking iron wheels which assaulted our ears and tore holes in the sturdy oak of the parquet floor. Twenty minutes before a despatch was due to go to the railway station the overseer would blow shrill blasts on his little whistle. There would follow a period of intense activity, christened 'organised chaos', with all taking their various parts. Trolley and skip pushers, sorters, baggers, tiers, sealers and 'holler-outers'. Sorters whipped sorted letters from frames, tied them in bundles with stout string and a quick-release knot; labelled them with labels bearing the office of despatch and delivery, then signed and date-stamped the labels – a device to ensure that missorters could be quickly traced and brought to disciplinary account. Letter bundles of two sizes, 'shorts and flats', ordinary letters and the larger business ones were hurled with packets into their appropriate bags. Registered items were bagged off in smaller green bags which were separately sealed and then placed in the final bag of each office of delivery. All labelled bags were whipped off the iron frame, tied with string, sealed with hot wax or lead, and piled in pyramids for checking.

'Calling' or 'hollering' baffled recruits, and even ancient sorters who had recently been transferred from offices elsewhere, on account of the local language. One sorter would call out the names from the bag labels as the overseer ticked them off his Despatch Register. Invariably, the place names would be translated.

'Eight final for all the fours!'

To the common tongue this meant that eight bags of His Majesty's mail were about to be despatched from Woking to Portsmouth. 'All the fours' was rhyming slang for 'Pompey Whores', the sailor's name for Portsmouth. There were other names – far less polite – for other places.

As soon as the overseer was satisfied that no bag had been overlooked from the scheduled despatch, he would hand over his mail to the Station Messenger, a postman with much gold braid on his cheese-cutter hat, who gave loud orders, assumed the air of a Grenadier RSM, and instructed a minor army of inferior postmen to escort himself and the mail to the station, to load the bags into various guard's vans.

Old Bill, one messenger, put a foot wrong one night. He had been in hospital for some time during which Woking Station had undergone reconstruction. As was his duty, he marched his men and the mail to the station, searched for mailbags in the guard's vans of trains standing at the platforms, and commanded that they should be taken back to the sorting office for our sorting attention. He was not quite up to scratch with the new geography of Woking Station, but began to learn about it the minute we brought back a large load of mail and called out the names from the labels – unfortunately, in reverse order. Salisbury the superintendent searched his 'Arrivals Register'. His brow became more furrowed than usual.

'Where the hell did you get that lot from? We are not due to receive mail from those offices at this time o' night!'

It transpired that Bill had marched his men down one platform to load the mail, then marched them through the new subway, and had taken out the same mail from the other side of the guard's van. We had to work even harder that night. Sometimes we had time to gulp down a cup of tea, but on this night we were tea-less.

SIX

Christmas Casuals

To me there seemed a clearly defined three-tiered caste hierarchy abiding in Woking sorting office, which was determined by the method of entry into the service. The majority were ex-boy messengers originally recruited to deliver telegrams. Because their fathers had been P.O. employees of some kind, they seemed content to hope to survive – first for the morning tea break, and ultimately until pension time. In the meantime they graduated to postmen and then to sorting clerks. The Writing Room fraternity were products of public schools who had passed the Civil Service examinations, wore their school colours on ties and blazers, and on their faces a look of superiority and contempt for the lowest caste, the 'untouchables' recruited at a mature age from the navy, army and air force. Seldom promoted, always allocated the worst duties and most irksome shifts – and their annual summer leave in April or October – the latter were the liveliest and most human.

Christmas was levelling time, when all had to muck in and become humanised. About a fortnight before, when seasonal cards were posted to distant lands, long queues appeared in the sorting office before the executives. Our sorting strength had to be supplemented by the temporary employment of Christmas casuals. Youths from schools and colleges were engaged as sorters and for door-to-door delivery duties. Older men from various walks of life were given the more menial tasks, bag opening, sealing, and packet and parcel sorting. Retired shopkeepers, who had experience in handling money and accountancy, were given the responsibilities of the registered cage – a kind of wire-netting hen coop wherein were received and despatched all registered items.

Christmas was an eye-opener.

About ten days before the peak, masses of mail poured in from sub-Post Offices, distant offices and pillar boxes, in constant streams. It did not seem possible that such a mass could be sorted and despatched before the next Christmas, let alone the one due. And in the meantime the casuals had to be given instructions, and were issued with brassards and bicycles and hosts of warnings about the safe custody and importance of the mail.

Overseers wore two watches apiece, synchronised them every five seconds and kept sharp eyes on the motley throng who had come to help us. Long established sorters told humorous stories about the antics of previous casuals. One old chap had been employed on the packet frame, sorting those which were too big for the letter frames but did not qualify as parcels. Although over sixty-five, he put the young professionals to shame. Mountains of packets seemed to dissolve or evaporate as old Edwin got mobile. His dress was somewhat unorthodox. His boots had once been South African field boots, but Edwin had turned them into ankle boots by chopping the long tops off with his bill hook. His braces were strips of canvas, whose frayed edges merged into the fluffiness of his pullover. The braces held up a pair of superfine khaki trousers, once worn (Edwin said) by the Prince of Wales. There was not a button on those princely pants. The braces were attached to them with two-inch wire nails. Although Edwin wore on his pullover the blue badge of the Temperance Society, his breath smelled of beer. He was so conscientious that he never took full advantage of his forty-minute dinner break. Instead, he used to shuffle off to the Railway Arms, sink a couple of swiftish pints, then return to his frame and resume sorting like a demon possessed with his left hand as he crammed bits of cheese roll into his mouth with his right.

When the Christmas rush was nearing its end, the overseer approached Edwin. 'You have done a good job. Such a good one that the boss has decided to keep you on a bit longer than the others. It's only temporary, mind you, but if you want to stay another month you can!'

'Thankee, matey!' said Edwin. 'Can do with a few bob at my age!'

The overseer stooped to pick up odd packets which had fallen from bags over-brimming with mail. He glanced at the addresses. To his surprise they bore no relationship to the names painted over the bags from which they had fallen. He sidled up to the whirlwind sorter and looked over his shoulder – just in time to see another packet put into the wrong bag.

'Just a minute, old chap. Don't get flustered because I'm talking to you. Have a bit of a blow. You've put some in the wrong bags. You'll have to be more careful about the addresses.'

'Addresses!' snorted Edwin. 'Ain't no good me lookin' at no addresses, matey . . . I can't bloody-well read!'

But the industrious Edwin had been hard at it for almost a fortnight. Just filling up His Majesty's mail bags.

On the previous Christmas a dapper young gentleman of Welsh extraction, who had managed a local shop so poorly that it had had to be sold, was entrusted with the registered cage. His job was to ensure that all registered items were put into their bags before despatch, and then to tick off the number of bags per postal town, per despatch. In the early hours of the morning, the overseer noticed that the Medhurst bag still hung alone from the frame.

'Mr Morgan, you have not sent the Medhurst,' he yelled.

'Sorry, I was just about to send it, sir.'

The overseer pulled letter bundles from the bag, and to his dismay found most of them bore date stamps three or four days old.

'When did you last send the Medhurst, Morgan?'

'Oh, I see, sir. Not since I took the job. You see, sir, the bag isn't full now, sir!'

Each Christmas one sorter was given a special job known as RLB, the Returned Letters Branch, or 'deads'. The object of the exercise was to open letters addressed to Father Christmas or Santa Claus from children who might have included money or postal orders to pay for their toys. If the address was given, the money would be returned to the sender. If there was money, but no address, the money would be sent to a charity. If the letters contained neither money nor addresses – there being no known postal circulation for 'Santa Claus, Reindeer Land' – they would be stacked away for ultimate destruction by the Post Office boiler furnace.

But one day there came a letter to the 'deads' which bore an unusual address, 'To God, c/o GPO'.

Distressed by its contents, the RLB sorter contravened instructions. He brought it to the staff retiring room where sorters were snatching a hasty meal, and read it aloud.

'Listen to this, lads . . . I reckon we ought to have a whip round.'

The letter came from an aged widow who required help from the Almighty. She was in arrears with her rent, lacked clothes and fuel, and her prospects of having a Christmas dinner were dim. She asked God for £3. This would pay her rent, buy her coal and a shawl, and something to eat.

The whip round produced £2 14*s*, enough to buy a Christmas card, a postage stamp and £2 10*s* in postal orders. The reply was duly despatched.

Early in the New Year another letter arrived in the 'deads'. It thanked God for his help and a happy Christmas, but also invited to the Almighty's attention that she had asked for £3 and had received only £2 10*s*. 'In future, please register your letters. The P.O. thieves have stolen ten shillings.'

Bridget hailed from Connemara. For years she had kept a shop where she sold food for pets, mostly birds. For years she had received from her native Ireland a fat turkey for Christmas. For several days before this Christmas she had come to the public counter, demanding that a search be conducted throughout the length and breadth of the sorting office to find her turkey. Searches were made, but no turkey came to light. On Christmas Eve she demanded to see the Postmaster 'Giniril', to complain that the Post Office staff had stolen her turkey. She was handed the complaint form. On Boxing Day she attended once more, complete with completed complaint form and a newspaper-wrapped parcel, and demanded to see the counter supervisor. The counter supervisor emerged from his den. Bridget handed over the form and the parcel, and began . . .

'I will sue the bloody lot o' yez. Six days I've been comin' to this place arskin' for me turkey from Ireland. What have yez got to say now? Open the parcel!'

The supervisor opened the parcel.

'Madam, these appear to be turkey's legs. Have you a complaint to make?'

'Complaint, is it! I had bully beef for me Christmas dinner, I did. On Christmas I was starved, I was. I went to me friend's house to a party on Christmas noight, and when I gets home I finds them legs hangin' on me door knocker, and a pack o'yelping dogs eatin' themselves sick on me Christmas dinner!'

Enquiry revealed that a guard's van had been shunted into a siding. In it were several bags of mail. A casual postman had tried his best to deliver the turkey, but Bridget was at the party. Being a Christian, if not a good postman, he hung the turkey to the door knocker of Bridget's abode. She was lucky that the dogs were small, otherwise the legs would not have been left. But once again the sorters came to the aid of the deprived, and bought Bridget a turkey. Like many of the sorters and postmen, she had her Christmas dinner on Boxing Day. And all was forgiven.

SEVEN

Deadlock and Wedlock

BECAUSE the fare from Woking was roughly half the fare from Aldershot, I was able to visit Vera at Golders Green more often, but not when I was on night work. On occasional weekends she would come to Woking and we would walk the Commons and pine woods on Sunday afternoons. One day I was bold enough to invite her to my Woking digs, but said nothing to Mrs Timms who was spending the day at Weybridge. I bought a few flowers for my room and dusted under my bed where bits of fluff were out of Mrs Timms's reach. She returned just as I was pouring tea for Vera. Her eyes flashed, she pretended to be hospitable and pleased to see Vera. We had not used the bed, but Mrs Timms suspected the worst and said so, next day. It was then that I decided to leave Holmside, but I had nowhere to go. One night I made the finest proposal of marriage in romantic history.

'Vera . . . if I can find a room with a bed will you come and dust under it?'

Her eyes told me. The bed was in a pleasant flat in Maybury, which we appeared to use alternately. When Vera was about to retire to bed it was time for me to go to work. When I returned to sleep, Vera would be up and about to get my breakfast. I was prompted to apply (through the usual channels) for transfer to any Post Office which had a vacancy for a Sorting Clerk and Telegraphist whose working hours permitted regular eating and sleeping. But Woking was reluctant to release folk for transfer (no one in his right mind would swop), and I was a long way down the list of applicants and had to wait my turn. Later we moved to a nice house in Eve Road, sharing the tenancy with another young married couple who, like us, could not afford to rent a whole house on P.O. wages. My son John was born in Eve Road, and for this important delivery the Post Office waxed benevolent and granted me two hours' leave.

'Get back for the night mail!'

Shortly afterwards I learned that my application for transfer had been approved and I was offered a vacancy for a Sorting Clerk and Telegraphist at Hayes, Middlesex. We found a house at Hatton Cross, Feltham, Middlesex and moved in with our own furniture, purchased on the never-never from a firm in Old Street. I had to buy a bicycle and used it to short-cut across the site now occupied by London (Heathrow) Airport. Gangs of Irish labourers were putting down those great triangular concrete runways which had spelt the finish of nurseries, smallholdings, greenhouses and broad acres rich with fruit trees. There were marquees and caravans along the London–Bath Road, the preliminaries to the international airport, 'The Gateway to the World'.

More varied than at Woking, without night duties, but in drawn-out shifts, I found work more interesting. There was an instrument room, about 12 ft by 9 ft, with a teleprinter and a telephone; a public counter (for the peddling of postal orders to football fanatics), and a sorting office. From time to time I functioned at all these points of duty – except the one for which I had received specialist training.

'The trouble is, Mr Mays,' said Postmaster Hopkins, 'I daren't let you touch the teleprinter until you've had proper Post Office training. It was military training you had at Cardiff.'

I applied for teleprinter training and in under a week was

sent on a three-month course to the Central Telegraph Office, almost under the dome of St Paul's Cathedral. Not one word did I utter about my previous training. For weeks I sat at the 'Imperial' telegraph typewriter, groping beneath its shield like the other twenty novices. I might have got away with it had it not been for young Kitty. She had applied for temporary transfer from Cardiff and happened to pass through the training school.

'What are you doing here? Are you on a refresher course?'

I told her the story, she promised to say not a word, but she had been overheard.

Next morning at the time of the daily test, I typed out 120 telegrams within an hour with only two errors. I had beaten the trainee's record, had created a precedent, an unforgivable offence in the walks of the civil service. A letter was sent to Postmaster Hopkins.

'It is understood that Mr Mays has received training at Cardiff. He is an expert telegraphist and requires no further training.'

The expert telegraphist reported for duty at 0800 hours the following Monday and inspected the Instrument Room. Everything necessary for transmitting and receiving telegrams was present and correct.

With a flick of the thumb I rotated the wooden wheel which whirled in water to moisten the adhesive side of the 3A tape. I fitted on my right index finger the thimble with the edge for cutting off the tape. There were batches of telegraph forms waiting to have messages gummed on to them. I flexed my well-trained fingers, switched the teleprinter to 'local', and typed a few words. After all my trials and tribulations, I was about to be a telegraphist.

The telephone rang. I picked up the receiver. A somewhat haughty voice said, 'This is Osborne of Southall, who is that?'

'This is Mays of Hayes,' said I.

There was a click as the receiver was put back on its cradle at the Southall end. Twenty minutes later, Postmaster Hopkins shuffled into the Instrument Room. 'Did you answer the telephone a little while ago?'

'Yes, why?'

'There has been a complaint. You have been facetious to Mr Osborne, the Assistant Head Postmaster.'

I did not reply. The teleprinter was chattering away, and I started to gum up my first Post Office telegrams.

With Arthur Briden, Bill Gomm, Jerry Dobson and Rex Winson, I took turns in teleprinting from that time on. But Postmaster Hopkins always regarded me with a shifty eye. He tried to get his revenge at Christmas 1937. In all I had worked ninety-four hours in one week. First, I had to cycle from Hatton Cross, a good thirty minutes, to open up the P.O. portals to let in the postmen for walk sorting at 0430 hours. During the day I moved from sorting office to public counter, to Instrument Room then back to the sorting office to send off the single daily despatch at 2230 hours. At 2235 hours I moved to the exit door and with my hand on the door-knob said, 'Goodnight.'

'You can't go yet, Mr Mays,' said Hopkins. 'We've got a van load in from Southall.'

'I have been here for over ninety hours. I am hungry and tired. If I don't go now I will have to be introduced to my family, whom I have not set eyes upon this week.'

'I shall have to give you a warning,' said Hopkins. 'The exigencies of the service distinctly state that officers can be kept on when required. If you insist on going home, I shall suspend you from duty.'

'You don't make sense, Mr Hopkins,' said I. 'You cannot afford to let me have time to eat and sleep, yet you can afford to suspend me from duty. I am going home. Goodnight!'

And then Hoppy got in a good one.

'All right, then. If you go you won't get your overtime money until after Christmas.'

This was a body blow. We needed the money. I stayed until 0010 hours, when Providence intervened. Paddy, one of the P.O. engineers, entered the sorting office, carrying his little black Gladstone bag filled with tools. He asked for the key of the cable chamber, a large cellar-like place which extended beneath the whole area of the Post Office.

'Can I see your pass?' I asked.

'Pass!' thundered Paddy, 'I bloody-well work here. You know me, I was playin' darts with you last week in the Crown.'

'I've never set eyes on you before. Come in here.'

I opened the registered cage door and when Paddy entered I locked him in, from the outside.

'One bleat from you and I'll clock you one with these sealing presses,' said I. Paddy was furious, but silent. I dialled the postmaster's home number, and a sleepy voice said, 'Hopkins here, who is that?'

'Mays. I am still at work, but I need your advice. A man just entered the sorting office and demanded the keys of the cable chamber. He was carrying a black bag, spoke with a pronounced Irish accent, and because the Irish have been blowing up pillar boxes I have locked him in the cage. Shall I call the police?'

'No, no, no. Not the police. Is he violent? I'm coming down, hold on there.'

Hoppy did not radiate officialdom in pyjamas and dressing-gown. He looked quite scared, until he saw Paddy.

'Goodness, gracious me! You know him, he's one of the engineers. You've got me out of bed because I kept you on. You'll hear more about this.'

I apologised, stating that the long hours might have affected my vision, and let Paddy free.

After Christmas, Hoppy sent me the official form, one which demanded explanations about my un-civil service behaviour. My reply stated that I had acted in the best interests of the General Post Office, and followed with a complaint about working over ninety-six hours in one working week – without appreciation or consideration. Unfortunately for Hoppy, he sent my reply to Regional Headquarters, King George V Building. To my delight I received a letter from the Regional Director – complimenting me on my devotion to duty, my presence of mind and concern for safeguarding P.O. property. The postmaster also received a letter, which took him severely to task for making me work such long hours. He used that letter to get his revenge. Not once did he allow me to perform overtime duties – even when I could have done with the money.

With the increasing dimensions of Vera's girth, there began a need for an increase in wages. The prospects of earning more in the Post Office were dim, so on 22 June 1938 I enlisted in the Supplementary Reserve, No. 48 Teleprinter Operating Section, 2 Line of Communication Signals, at Balham. For attending the Drill Hall once a week, and going to camp for a fortnight once a year, I was entitled to £30 per annum. Everything helped.

In the early hours of 11 July 1938 – after I had returned about midnight after a hard day's work – Vera was most restless in our bed. Through a haze of sleep I heard odd moans and complaints that she must have eaten something that disagreed with her stomach. She also thought she might be nearing her time, and kept waking me to say so. I told her to make up her mind, either to defecate or produce a child. This statement was made in the roughest of ex-trooper's terms, and produced signs which were unmistakable. I mounted my bicycle and tore off to the District Nurse's house in Feltham, a mile and a bit away. The nurse was abed. Her motor-car was out of sorts and off the road. She did not fancy riding on my cross-bar, but loaded me with bales of cotton wool and a box with red rubber tube things and told me to get off home while she borrowed a car from a neighbour. As I cycled at a pretty good lick across

Feltham Park, my bicycle chain broke, and I had to walk. Lights were on all over the house. Nurse Collins had beaten me to it and had just finished tying a knot in the umbilical cord of my new son Glyn. The house was full of steam, blood and noise – and a great happiness.

Each week I used to buy a tool of some kind. Sometimes it would be for the garden, a pair of shears, a fork, or a spade. Sometimes I would buy pliers, solder, flex and insulating tape – to help me in my money-earning hobby of repairing wireless sets for friends and neighbours. I had no workshop or bench, but used the kitchen table.

'Why not get some planks and build a bench in the box-room?' said Vera. 'You've burnt holes in the carpet and table with that soldering iron, and I've nearly been electrocuted twice.'

I gave the matter thought, but that was all.

About a month later, Vera was quite ill. She had run a sliver of wood from the broom handle into a finger which became badly infected. Her arm had swollen considerably and the doctor had probed with his lance to get out the wood, but with little success. Clarice, Vera's sister, arrived from Wales and decided to take her back to her parents for a bit, to have a rest and to get better treatment.

I missed her very much, and the boys, and had time on my hands. One morning my friend Nobby Clark, the Post Office storeman, took me to his stores. He pointed to an old writing-table of solid oak; six feet long, three feet wide, with three oak drawers, all beautifully dove-tailed, with a brass lock and key for each drawer. Its top was covered with red leather and ink stains.

'They want to get shot of this to make room, Spike,' said Nobby. 'Write to old Hoppy and make him an offer. With a bit of elbow grease and some wax polish it will shine like a shilling up a sweep's arse. If you don't want it yourself, you'd be able to flog it for a tenner.'

I did not write to the postmaster, I spoke to him.

'You'll have to write to the P.O. Stores Department, in triplicate. A copy to me, it has to come through your immediate superior, and a copy for yourself. Here's a franked envelope.'

I wrote . . .

> Post Office Stores Department,
> Mount Pleasant,
> London, EC1.
>
> I am informed that an old writing-table here is surplus to service requirement and is available for staff purchase. I would like to buy it.
>
> C. W. Mays (S.C. & T.),
> HAYES, Middlesex P.O.

One week later I was called to the postmaster's office and was introduced by Hoppy to a sartorially splendid civil servant complete with morning coat, striped trousers, bowler, brief case and brolly.

'This gentleman is from Headquarters, he's come to see you about buying that table.'

We trooped up the back stairs to the store room. The gentleman prodded the table top with his close-furled gamp.

'Is not this a fine table, Mr Mays?'

'Not bad,' said I.

'How much are you prepared to offer?'

'Fifteen bob.'

'Goodness, gracious me! Each lock is worth more than that!'

'I don't need locks or drawers. Just the top and the legs, to make a workbench.'

For a good five minutes he extolled the virtues of the table, insisting it would be sold in one piece or not at all. We argued. He would not lower his voice, and I would not raise my price. He looked at his watch . . .

'I have to go. Make me another offer!'

'Ten bob,' said I.

He looked very angry. 'Take it and be damned. It has to go, but it has cost the Department more than that for my fares.'

He gave me a receipt and flounced off. I looked at my table and thought what a bargain I'd got.

Because I had to work until 10.30 p.m. I arranged for one of the delivery van drivers to dump my table on what Vera called our front lawn – a patch of vetch-like grass about 18 ft by 12 ft. When I arrived home at 11.0 p.m. I could just make out the outlines of the table in the dark, standing wet and forlorn in the rain. I had not the heart to leave it out all night, and tried to take it through the front door; a noisy, cursing business which woke neighbours who complained. George Shankster, who lived next door, took pity and helped. We broke two banister rails and tore substantial strips off my new wallpaper. After taking the box-room door off its hinges we took the table inside and stood it flush against the wall, under the window where the light would shine through to light my endeavours. I sat at my writing-table and – without a mention of the damage – wrote a long letter to Vera about my bargain, saying that I would visit her next weekend.

Vera had got worse in Wales. Her arm was almost double its size and she was in great pain. She had been given injections, been poulticed from finger tips to armpit, and given all kinds of pills and medicines. In desperation we took her to Job, an old recluse who gathered herbs, made his own medicines and cured people of afflictions which had beaten the local doctors.

He lived in an old cottage at Fforestfach, midway between Loughor and Swansea. Great bunches of dried herbs hung from his picture rail. Bowls and dishes had been filled with the fruits and seeds of wild flowers, and there was a mixture of all their scents which hit the nostrils with a great fragrance. Job spoke in a mixture of excellent Welsh and deplorable English, but he had not a lot of time for words. He looked at Vera's swollen arm, squeezed her here and there, looked into her eyes, then got out an iron saucepan. In the saucepan he put a dollop of white vaseline, various helpings of herbs from various jam jars and basins, then placed the saucepan on his open fire. He looked at his grandfather clock and said not a word. Soon, a wonderful smell of the countryside filled the room.

With a putty knife he scraped up a generous portion of brown soft soap and put it into a jampot. He broke into words.

'Wash your hands with this twice a day, Cariad. Both hands. Dry in front of the fire. Not with a towel!'

He poured his mixture from the saucepan into an old brown jar, tied the top with a string handle, and put a disc of brown paper on top of the oily ointment.

'Rub it in gentle, mind you! Twice a day, after the wash.'

'How much?'

'Nuthin' now. When you are better, Cariad, give me somethin' for vaseline. Bore Da!'

The instructions were heeded. In three days pus poured. The splinter came with it, fully two inches long. In a week the roses were back in Vera's cheeks; but she stayed on in Wales to get back to health.

EIGHT

Gwlad y Gân (Land of Song)

ALTHOUGH I had worked in Cardiff as a mufti-clad soldier, I did not enjoy that city so much as the steel and coal towns and villages of Glamorganshire and Carmarthenshire. My heart used to leap in anticipation of meeting firm friends each time I dismounted from the London train at Swansea and paid one and threepence to the conductor of a red South Wales Transport bus; the return fare for a five and a half mile ride to 'Tyrcoed', 14, Belgrave Road, Loughor, Glamorganshire, the home of my wife's parents, Joe and Mary Jones.

I went there with Vera soon after we were married, and again for my Post Office leaves, but I managed to put a foot wrong twice on my first attendance at Moriah Chapel. The Reverend William John Lunt was a saintly-looking man with silvered locks and a voice as mellow as old gold. I sat between my sister-in-law Clarice and Vera, about to listen to soul-stirring Welsh hymns at the annual singing festival, the Gymanfa Ganu. We sat downstairs in the well of the chapel. In the galleries, twenty feet above us, were the choristers. Old men and boys, old women and girls, young men and maidens; a mixture of miners, steelworkers and all kinds of professional men, all bursting to sing.

Mr Lunt gave an address in his native tongue. For ten minutes he stood on his rostrum making quite pleasant noises like a musical rendering of a meteorological report in Chinese;

which conveyed nothing to me but his sincerity. The conductor crept into the act. He stood up, looked up to the galleries, and raised his baton. The choristers stood up. I stood up. The only one standing downstairs.

'Sit down, you fool . . . only the choir!' hissed Clarice, as Vera crimsoned with shame. From my off-rear I heard a woman say to a colleague, '*Nid ydoedd yn deall, Sais ydyw!*' Roughly translated this meant, 'He wouldn't understand, he's English.' But I did not get the meaning until I asked my mother-in-law, just after I had done the other wrong thing.

After the service Mr Lunt stood at the chapel door to chat with members of his congregation. He came over to me and shook hands with great warmth.

'Congratulations on marrying Vera. Welcome to Moriah!'

I offered him a cigarette – on a Sunday, on hallowed ground! They still talk of it in Loughor. From then on I took lessons in Welsh from Vera by waking her at odd sleepless times in the night to ask her about words and phrases. I was determined to find out what these 'foreigners' were saying about me.

It was an enchanting linguistic adventure to sit next to Joe Jones on his old oak settle ('the skew') trying to pick out odd words. Each time I turned up all the relatives and friends turned up, and that friendly Christian home would be filled with married couples, the children of my parents-in-law: Gwynfor and Florrie, Trevor and Olive, Clarice and Jack, Ivor and Irene, Islwyn and Ethel. Those with children brought them, of both sexes and various sizes, to add to my delight and confusion, for they spoke mostly in Welsh.

Best of all I liked visiting the Globe, a small pub on the Llanelli Road which stood opposite Moriah Chapel. We did not do a lot of drinking. One or two pints of Buckley's, or Felinfoel ale would last the evening. It was not fully licensed, just a beer house with two rooms, the Tap and the Discussion. With my brothers-in-law I went to the Tap, to play darts with their friends. With my father-in-law it was always to the

Discussion, the meeting place of tradesmen, teachers, doctors, mine managers and the upper crust of the local steel industries.

I felt very much at home there and was reminded of the Bonnett at Reuben's Corner. At the Globe there were discussions about work in mines, roller mills, tin-plate works, politics and philosophy, recitals of poetry, and gossip about friends and neighbours. The Welsh have a flair for self education and are great readers. There were stories in the appearances of these fine men. Gnarled hands and tattoos of coal stain told of hard work over long years, eyes still carried the scars of worry and care from the years of the depression. Like our old farmhands, each man had a nickname, from 'Dai the Milk' to 'Tom the Meat'.

I was invited to visit all the local works, to go deep into the mines, to choir practices and on visits to the 'spookies'. I went to them all and learned a great deal and used to think of those kindly men whose feet clattered under my bedroom window down Belgrave Road on their return from the late shift. Above the boot bashings were the incessant thumps and clatterings of Llanelli's steel plants, as powerful steel rollers kneaded white hot ingots into fiery red ribbons of steel.

Glyn Davies, works manager of the Bynea Steel Works, a strict disciplinarian and a skilled metallurgist, was my particular friend. He took me to his plant on many an occasion, and explained in detail the many processes of making steel. With dark blue goggles shielding my eyes from the glare I watched the tapping of the vast furnaces; saw the molten steel pour like lava into the ingot moulds; then helped to charge a furnace with a heavy unwieldy shovel as long as a cavalry lance. One day he took me walking across the flats of the River Loughor's estuary to Penclawdd, the village where he was born, the home of the cockle women who rode out on donkeys at high tide to net their harvests of cockles and 'bara lawr' (laver bread), a blackish, greenish, cow-dungish delicacy made from seaweeds, which put one's taste buds on their mettle to make the world's best bacon (Welsh) even more palatable. Glyn spoke of his little village with great pride.

'Hayden Tanner, the international rugger star, was born here. But, Cedric, this little spot has the Welsh record for higher education. Almost every child born here has received university education.' He pointed to the beach where hordes of rough-clad, gipsy-like women were boiling cockles in sturdy iron cauldrons. 'Those women work like beavers to send their children to good schools. It is almost part of their religion.'

Poor Glyn. His own child Patricia, the joy of his heart, died soon after she gained her Fellowship in Philosophy at Aberystwyth. Glyn did not live long after that blow, he seemed to lose the knack for living.

My friend William James is in his grave too. He used to take me to the mines and show me how men who walked five miles from Swansea to the pithead had still to crawl and creep for half a mile or more to reach the coal face. Their wage, which was based on starting time, did not begin until they reached the coal face. There were no baths or Miners' Welfare Centres. James was the manager of the Miners' Rescue Station for South Wales. He told me of the maiming and killing by cruel rocks and explosions underground; of the weeping of women above ground, and the singing of men as they hacked with their picks in blackness.

I had a great love for my father-in-law, a truly remarkable man who, for the greater part of his life, worked with steel as a rollerman; turning and cutting hot sheets of steel into various thicknesses as the great wheel turned in the centre of the works to dictate the working speed. Joe Jones invented a gadget to eliminate some superfluous motion of the rolling process and had saved his firm many thousands of pounds. When he became crippled and had to retire prematurely they were kind to him. For a few years they paid him his wages in full, then gave him a modest pension.

After months in hospital Joe's hip had had to be locked by

surgery and silver pins. In consequence one leg was a good three inches shorter than the other. The supreme optimist, Joe was convinced that even though surgeons had failed he, one day, would succeed in levelling up his legs. To achieve this he resorted to the most extraordinary devices, some of which I witnessed with alarm. One day I caught him in his workshop. The heel of his big boot – the one padded inside to even up the short leg a bit – was set firmly in the iron vice with Joe's foot still in it. He was hurling himself backwards to the floor full-weight, trying to stretch his leg. Without useful results he spent hundreds of pounds on quack medicines and well advertised panaceas. His costliest purchase was an electric contraption which worked on the lines of diathermy. It was a moleskin-like pad containing three elements, and had to be connected to the mains by a long lead bearing a three-point switch, for low, medium or high. Joe had been inspired to buy this because 'Faith' failed. It was not Joe's personal faith which had let him down. Months before he had taken to visiting a faith healer at Llanelli. I accompanied him on two occasions and was introduced to the faith healer, Mr Toft. A medium-sized room had been converted into a chapel which contained a diminutive altar, a brass cross and a brace of brass candlesticks. The most prominent feature was a large collecting box. The *modus operandi* was on the religious side. Prayers were prayed, and blessings were broadcast left, right and centre. Finally, attention was invited to the presence of the collecting box, and to earnest thought, hope and prayer – on an individual basis – at home.

As was his custom, Joe observed the instructions devoutly, but still one leg remained shorter than the other. Then the blow fell. Toft the healer died. Joe was most upset that the spiritual physician had failed to cure himself, and took to visiting the 'spookies'; those who dabbled in Spiritualism, who dimmed their lights and sat in dark rooms to sing rousing Welsh hymns – in uncanny whispers.

This was a great shock to his wife Mary, a most religious and God-fearing lady whose Bible was seldom out of her reach. She implored him to eschew such practices, to leave the dead alone. But one night Joe returned home from the 'spookies' frightened out of his wits. Mary took him to task, but he would not heed her.

'You must listen. I've had a message for you, from the beyond!'

He settled himself on the old skew and asked questions.

'Mary, was there a brooch? Did Margaretta have a brooch?'

This was even a greater blow to Mary, and she told him how, long before they had met, her father had sent her a gold brooch from America. When her sister Margaretta started courting, she had lent her the brooch, but on condition that if Mary married and had a girl, Margaretta must return it. Their first child was a boy, Gwynfor, so Mary did not bother about the brooch and had never mentioned it, not even to her husband. She asked how he had come to know about it when she had not said a word to anyone but her dead sister.

Joe told her of the medium who had arrived that night from London. A total stranger to the locality, she had hurled herself into a trance and had spoken to him about a brooch 'in the voice of Margaretta'. This astonishing story so upset Mary that Joe vowed never to visit the 'spookies' again, and he never did. Instead, to find solace, or to lengthen his leg, he resorted to his electrical device – with increasing frequency.

One afternoon he sat on his settle with the pad strapped firmly to his hip. Never a believer in half measures, he set the switch to 'high'. His walking stick, which he used to switch the mains on and off, fell to the floor beyond his reach after he switched on. There was nothing particularly significant about the dropping of his stick until a visitor arrived.

Healer Toft's deputy, who had assumed full command since his master had passed on, was seeking new clients. He stayed for a good hour, and said how flushed and hot Joe looked and that he must be running a temperature. After another cup or so of tea he departed. Not wishing to disclose to the faith healer that he was employing electrical aids, unable to reach his stick to switch the thing off, poor Joe had endured an agony of burning. Skin peeled off his hip in the same shape and dimensions of the pad when Joe tore it off. It was not used again.

But one night I decided to attend the 'spookies' on the occasion of their annual general meeting. After the Secretary had read his report the Treasurer rendered his, to cause quite a bit of merriment. He acknowledged receipt of various donations, including 'two doublers' (two twenty packets of Woodbine cigarettes). 'We have also received a donation from the Ymca,' said he, believing it to be a Welsh word. It was from the YMCA.

Fat and fierce-looking, with an accent peculiar to North Wales, a woman rose and introduced a medium who might well have been her twin sister. The shapes and sounds were identical. The medium glanced round the hall and began to deliver messages from the spirit world. Warnings about catching cold, failing to attend meetings, and not taking pills prescribed by doctors. She picked on me.

'There are doubters here!' Her forefinger sought me out. 'Listen, now. I will convince you. I have not seen you before, have I?'

I shook my head.

'You are from London, the civil service!'

I nodded.

'Wheels within wheels. You have two enemies who are jealous of you. Something to do with letters, it is.'

She closed her eyes, shook like an aspen, put on a most ferocious expression and began.

'I've got a message for you from J.M. He was old, had a beard, and helped you when you were little by dragging you from the water. He is helping you now, from beyond.'

That ended my message. I was not impressed, but next time I went home to Ashdon I told the story to my mother, who was most impressed.

'J.M., with a beard. That's your uncle Jasper Miller, the gamekeeper. Been dead twenty years now. Wait a minute!'

She got out our faded album. Inside was a picture of a bearded man pulling a child from a puddle. The child was wearing a pinafore and a sash. It was my uncle Jasper, and the child was me. Apparently we were just about to have our photographs taken when I strayed and fell in the mud. Mother accused me of making it all up, saying I had seen the photograph years before. Rather than disturb her peace of mind I laughed it off, but I too have not been to the 'spookies' any more.

Tom Rees, the local butcher, broad as he was long, red of face and bulging with fatness and joviality under an ugly tweed hat and canopies of blue and white striped apron, loved the countryside and knew much about it. Sometimes he took me motor riding to witness the famous sheep dog trials at Penllegaer, where farmers and shepherds congregated in betting droves from counties remote. It was an education to see those shaggy dogs herding wayward sheep into pens and folds they had not seen before. Whistle blasts from the shepherd, but never a word of command, and the dogs did the rest as the punters took stock of their stop-watches. Afterwards, we would retire to delightful old inns, for a hearty meal and the inevitable sing-song.

Tommy 'Paris House' Davies earned his nickname because he kept a draper's shop of that name in nearby Gorseinon. The shyest and kindest man of my experience he spoke always in confidential whispers as if fearful of being overheard. He had enjoyed his business visits to London, but vowed never to go again.

'Daren't go, man. They know me. Blotted my copybook!'

It was nothing really serious. He had gone to a theatre and

had laughed so hard that his ill-fitting dentures landed in the lap of a lady two rows in front. Torches had been brought into play, and Tommy was under floodlight when the teeth were returned.

Wee Ewart Rees was a miner. Barely five feet tall and every inch of him stained with coal scars, his claim to local fame was the speed of his speech. Words rattled from him like bursts of machine-gun fire.

'Yes, yes! We know about Ewart, boyo. It's a funny tongue he's got. Stitched down in the middle, not at the back like ours. Clacks at both ends!'

It was a joy to hear Ewart speaking, but it was angelic to hear him singing 'Calon Lân'.

My brother-in-law Gwynfor won prizes for his tenor singing. An excellent fisherman, he was also a first-class shot. But there was one shooting he would like to forget. He took me on a brief visit to his father-in-law who had a small farm five miles off the road near Llanmorlais. Gwynfor came sidling up to me with two 12-bore double-barrelled guns, and gave large winks to indicate secrecy. He whispered, 'Quick, Cedric. A covey of partridges has just gone down in that stubble near the chapel.'

We crept down hedgerows and took up our position in a ditch. The heads of the birds were bobbing about twenty feet away.

'One barrel at 'em now, and one when they're on the wing . . . Now!'

We fired together. The birds rose. I knew as I pressed the trigger for the second shot that this was not the flight of partridges. But in four shots we bagged five birds. Complete with rings and tallies they were tame pigeons. Every clue was removed. Feathers and fluff were plucked from the stubbles. On our return to Loughor, the birds were handed to Mrs Morgan, who soon hid them from further view – under a pie crust.

Sometimes we would go off from Swansea on the tram which ran to Mumbles to visit the lovely, natural bays, Langland, Bracelet, Three Cliffs, and if time permitted we went further west to Portynon, Worm's Head, and to the sweeping beauty of Rhossili Bay. I always found peace and contentment in that unspoiled spot. Just the languid swell and gentle breaking of white-maned rollers as they queued to lap and kiss the golden sands. Above me the mewing of plaintive seagulls. There were no other sounds. My feet were muffled by that rare grass. Short, fine and yellow it thrives on sandy loam and provides a sound-deadening carpet for the Rhossili Downs, the highest point in glorious Gower, and for the cliffs that seem to parachute themselves into the sea. To walk on that rare Alpine Whitlow Grass and to listen to the sound of sea and birds is joy. Each time I do it, and it is usually once a year, I feel convinced that one of the best love songs of Wales had its birth at Rhossili.

AR LAN Y MOR

Ar lan y môr mae rhosys cochion,
Ar lan y môr mae lili gwynion,
Ar lan y môr mae 'nghariad inne
Yn cysgu'r nos a chodi'r bore.

ON THE SEA-SHORE

On the sea-shore are red red roses,
On the sea-shore are whitest lilies,
On the sea-shore my love is pining
Asleep at night, at dawn awaking.

I did not always find peace in Wales. Where the railway bridge runs over the River Loughor, the natural boundary between Glamorganshire and Carmarthenshire, there is a spot known as Loughor Lido, the children's paradise. It is but a small strip of beach where in summer the children are almost as thick as the grains of sand, and noisier than the combined steelworks of Loughor, Gorseinon and Llanelli. I used to troop down there some afternoons with my two sons, John and Glyn, and my young nephews, Peter and Michael, the sons of Gwynfor and Florrie; Alwyn, the son of Ivor and Irene; and Michael, the son of John and Clarice. It was sheer torture. The minute I stripped off – we undressed in full public view – I would be subjected to sandstorms fiercer by far than those I had endured in Egypt. If I was sufficiently ill-inspired to prostrate myself, I would be buried, stamped upon, and have sand-castles built on my belly and chest. There was only one means of escape. I used to tie up my clothes in a bundle, grip the bundle with my teeth, jump into the River Loughor, and swim across to the Carmarthenshire side to sunbathe. But the tribe would find me out when they had their fill of noise, sunshine and sand-blasting, and they would join hands with me and sing all the way to Tyrcoed, Belgrave Road, where Mam would have the table laid with bowls of Penclawdd cockles, home-baked bread, and butter the colour of marigolds.

'He's a cheat, Mam . . . Uncle Cedric swam over and went to sleep.'

NINE

Counter Measures

AFTER A FEW months I was switched to the public counter. The moment I ceased to deal with postal and telegraph matters my title of Sorting Clerk and Telegraphist was changed to Counter Clerk and Telegraphist. The Hayes public counter was a peculiar place, in more ways than one.

Heavily industrialised, this straggling town of about 65,000 was unable to provide the labour force required by the large factories of Electrical and Musical Industries, Fairey Aviation, Kraft Cheese, Nestlé and many others. Each working day, including Saturdays, saw a mass influx of non-residents from remote areas who could not get to their local Post Offices because they were not open when they left for work, and would be closed before they returned. Consequently, a Post Office which had never been designed or staffed adequately to cope with the residents of Hayes, had to try to cope with a daily invasion.

Time and again representation was made to the official side by the local officers of the Union of Post Office Workers. This problem was common to a number of industrialised provincial towns, but it did not seem possible to enlighten or convince the Headquarters' planners of the dearth of staff and services. The top brass called meetings, drew district maps, stuck coloured pins and little flags on them, then called more meetings. After a number of these had been negotiated with no outward and visible sign of action or progress, someone would suggest opening yet another sub-Post Office, of which Hayes already had a dozen, mostly in the districts where customers were thin on the ground. These were run in various shops with sub-standard accommodation by non-professional sub-postmasters and sub-postmistresses, usually those who had retired from other forms of employment and had little or no training in Post Office affairs. Ill-paid for their responsibilities – even in those areas where demand for postal services was low – they seemed to concentrate their endeavours and attention on the more profitable aspects of their little shops; the sale of cigarettes, liquorice all-sorts and picture postcards.

When the residential and non-residential factory-employed masses emerged for lunch they made bee-lines for the main Post Office, hoping to catch the counter clerk's eye and buy stamps and postal orders within the forty-minute or one-hour lunch break. Many were disappointed. Queues were in battalion strength before each of the seven counter positions, one of them bearing the sign 'Closed'. The queuers were like cup final crowds refused entrance to the stands. Tempers were as short as the queues were long. Insults and abuse were hurled left, right and centre at young girls of sixteen or eighteen years of age who, for a wage of about 35*s* per week, were saddled with the responsibility of daily balancing a till containing £4,000 to £5,000 in official cash and stock.

There were separate positions for the various transactions. All licences, car, radio, dog and gun, together with money orders, were catered for at one position. There were three for savings bank, postal orders and stamps. Parcels, packages and telegrams were accepted at two points where postage and insurance stamps could be purchased. One position remained closed, to enable the staff to take turns to eat.

If a customer was sufficiently ill-inspired to require a money order, to put money in the savings bank and to send a telegram or post a parcel, he had to queue three times. Hence, there were cunning jockeyings for position, jostlings, nudgings and queue-jumping, followed by trooper-like cursings and occasional punch-ups for which the counter staff were always blamed.

I was once goaded into violence myself, over a £3 savings bank withdrawal. When a depositor presented his savings book to make a demand, he had to leave the book with the counter clerk who then handed over a Demand Form on which the account name and number, the amount required and the signature had to be written. The book was held to prevent fraudulent withdrawals by the easy copying of signatures. Unfortunately, because there were no pens or ink at the counter, the depositors had to write at the distant side of the office. By the time they had completed their clerical performances longer queues would have congregated, and it was seldom that depositors were allowed to reserve their positions.

My particular depositor was livid with rage because I would not allow him to retain his book while completing his withdrawal form. In a booming voice he said unkind things about my parents, and ended: 'You are an idle shower of bastards, the lot of you. If it wasn't for this grille,' he pointed to our lattice screen, 'I'd punch your bloody nose, mate!'

To the consternation of my impatient queue I closed and locked my till and confronted the aggressive one, on the public side of the counter.

'Now is your chance,' said I. 'There is no grille, mate.'

He lashed out, but I got in two good ones; one down, one up, and put him on his back. I dragged him through the main entrance and as he rose to his knees I planted on him a hefty kick. In seconds he was deluged with tomatoes, apples, onions, cherries and various greengrocery. I had kicked him under Tom Hall's stall. It took me some time to help Tom put his stall back to rights, but far longer to answer the letter of explanation demanded of me by the postmaster. I felt bound to explain that I resorted to fisticuffs only to defend the honour of the postmaster, whom I suspected was not a bastard. I was forgiven by the postmaster. The depositor did not call for his book for over a week. I handed it back the moment he apologised.

There were occasions when humour took over to brighten our lives. Arthur Willie Briden, a fellow counter clerk, and one who had an eye for the girls, was in fits of laughter one afternoon. A young lady who was as shy as she was pretty minced up to Arthur's position and said, 'Please can I have a form?'

'What sort?' replied Arthur. 'We've got fousands!'

'A nice pink one,' said she.

'Blimey! You've already got one, m'dear.'

'Don't be personal, or I shall report you. I want a form at once, I've been interfered with!'

It transpired that the little lady had trouble with her radio set, and wished to complain of electrical interference.

A nice old lady of sixty-plus pattered to the parcel acceptance point one morning and gingerly handed over a parcel. 'Don't hit it too hard with your stamping thing, dearie. Look at the handle I've made with my string. It's specially for the postman. I want him to carry it this way up. It's for me sister. She's a bit poorly, so I've made her a nice steak and kidney pie. It must be carried this way up 'cos the gravy ain't set yet.'

Inspection of the address revealed that some postman was expected to carry it by the nice string handle, all the way to Jarrow.

There were always problems about the completion of the many forms. Sometimes we would do the lot, to help the customer and to save time. We did not always get the same assistance from the public. One lady, when asked, 'Name, please?' replied, 'Spot.' She had just handed over 7*s* 6*d* for a dog licence.

Unlike that last half-hour before closing time in most English pubs, when complete strangers speak to each other, and sometimes open their mouths in song, the last hour before Post Office closing time would see a setting of chins and a tightening of lips. That perilous period known as balancing time was near.

Some factories released their employees at 5.0 p.m., others at 5.30. The door of our public office closed at 6.0 p.m. There were frantic bustlings, bumpings and borings on the public side, where queues of impatient customers hoped to catch stamps and postal orders before catching their trains to distant homes. Insults rained like manna from heaven, just at the time when nerves needed to be steady for the daily ordeal of balancing an intricate account within the official time limit, one hour. Each clerk was held responsible for his own account. It was the exception rather than the rule, even for old stagers, to arrive at a balance at the first attempt. Some would have a surplus, some a deficit. Perhaps just a few pence, maybe many pounds. But the account had to be checked and re-checked before reporting a loss or gain to the duty overseer, who usually became infuriated and regarded poor arithmetic as a personal affront to his lofty state, for the simple reason that he had to check the account himself before a 'counter loss form' could be issued. Perhaps, after spending half an hour in checking a short till, he would discover that the date had been added to a long list of savings bank deposits, and the Cash Locked Up was a mere £1,938 short. Whatever the outcome of the check, the result was always the same. Clerks had to pay a proportion of all losses, and any gains not claimed by the public were donated to benefit funds. Double checking by the clerk, followed by the overseer's check, ate away time. Often it would be eight o'clock and sometimes nine before the weary harassed clerk locked away his till, to learn with dismay that unless the local accounts officer discovered an error when he completed the main account next morning, which had to balance to the halfpenny for the Accountant General's Department each day, he would suffer a counter loss, a fine and an adverse report classified as a Minor Irregularity. Although Minor Irregularities were not permanently recorded in the officer's Principal Conduct Record, as were Major Irregularities and Serious

Irregularities, they were taken into account; oral warnings were given that when the time rolled round for him to receive his annual increment, the matter might be given due consideration. Habitual carelessness after oral warning might result in the increment being deferred. The counter clerk could not win. He would not be overjoyed because in failing to balance he worked an hour or two above the normal eight for nothing. Self-inflicted extended attendances did not qualify for overtime payment.

'Claim for Counter Loss' forms were dreaded. Form A catered for losses of less than 5*s*. Couched in officialese, they were already addressed to the Officer-in-Charge of the Counter. If the loss was authorised, the loser signed for the amount required to balance his till. But his attention was invited to exercise more care in future. If two or more losses occurred, even if the total amount was only 5*s* 6*d*, form B had to be completed by the supervising officer. If the loss exceeded 5*s*, yet another form was brought into action.

Confounded by the wealth that dwelt in my till, and not over-impressed by the wages paid to me to safeguard it, I was perhaps the world's worst counter clerk. In my first week I signed more counter loss forms for amounts above 5*s* than anyone else in Hayes. Had it not been for Gerry Hubbard, a Southall man promoted to overseer who kept a sharp look-out on my inferior performance, the Post Office Investigation Branch might have put their spies on me and I could have landed up in Wormwood Scrubs. But Gerry made a remarkable discovery about my popularity with postal order purchasers. I had failed to charge them the poundage. This amounted to a tidy sum. Postal orders ranged from 6*d* to £1, twenty-four denominations in all. We usually sold about 700 each and every day.

Anyway, I stuck to the counter, determined to get the hang of it, and I finally succeeded. Then I decided to apply for writing duties. Postmaster Hopkins breathed a sigh of great relief. In no time at all I was officially issued with a red bicycle, black Gladstone bag equipped with the Royal Cipher, and reams of instructions. I was appointed the local Post Office Enquiry Officer. In this capacity I cycled to outflung areas of Hayes to check up on folk who failed to renew their wireless licences; to ascertain that persons entitled to Post Office pensions were still living, and that their pensions were not being drawn by cunning relatives who had failed to inform the Postmaster-General of pensioners' deaths. I invaded factories, infiltrated into various industrial concerns to inspect parcels and packages damaged in the post, and produced letters typed in advance according to the official examples provided.

TEN

UPW

My first real encounter with the Union of Post Office Workers was in the staff retiring room of Hayes Post Office. Encrusted with rusty metal lockers, hooks and pegs for hats and coats and the capes of postmen it had a sink with ill-labelled taps, enamel-topped tables, and a dozen rickety chairs. It was the place where we counter clerks dodged the general public twice a day, to drink tea and tittle-tattle about grievances real or imagined and gossip about colleagues and seniors in rank. On this particular morning our room had been borrowed for an emergency union meeting. Two of our postmen, unestablished staff, had taken more than their quota of sick leave without producing medical certificates and had been discharged. Tempers were high, language low.

I was not then a member of the UPW. I could not spare the weekly membership fee of 6*d*. But because I had written a letter for the branch secretary a week or so earlier, I was asked to sit in and give my opinion, and to draft another letter. The first letter was about a postman who had lost a toe and had been granted modest financial compensation for about six months. The head office had written to say that the payment of compensation would cease forthwith because in the opinion of the experts the disability had ceased. I wrote to say that the toe was still absent and the disability was present. Payment was resumed.

After the emergency meeting I wrote to suggest that our

two postmen should be given a medical examination, otherwise we had no alternative but to put the matter into the hands of the press. Within a week the postmen were medically examined. Within a fortnight they were reinstated. Within three weeks I was elected Branch Secretary and Welfare Representative and began to take a lively interest in the official and domestic affairs of my colleagues, and read books on trade unions.

Most of the representation I had to make was petty in the extreme. I had to do battle for persons who were not God's gift to punctuality, for those who gambled and borrowed (and were caught at it), and for young ladies caught indulging in 'private occupations while on Duty'.

So were our miserable lives regulated. Each month we held a branch meeting. Protests were made about some of the outmoded rules; facts and figures were quoted about the time taken by postmen to deliver letters on their various walks, and the incidence of delay through dog-bites. Graphs, diagrams and charts were produced to indicate the growth of counter transactions. Complaints were made about undue officiousness of overseers, superintendents and postmasters. The branch became extremely lively, but unduly committee conscious. If something unusual appeared upon the agenda a sub-committee would be appointed to examine it and report at the next meeting. At the next meeting another sub-committee would be appointed, to examine and report upon the findings of the first sub-committee at the next meeting. And so it went on until the Annual General Meeting, when new officers were elected and votes were cast to determine who should be the delegate at the UPW annual conference. Once a quarter the staff representatives met the official representatives at the Whitley Council, when both sides from the offices of Southall, Greenford and Hayes endeavoured to reach agreement on points of policy, but seldom did so. Then the whole business would start again, with both sides writing long letters to their respective top brass at UPW Headquarters, Crescent Lane,

Balham and GPO Headquarters, King Edward Building, St Martin's-le-Grand. On one occasion I wrote no fewer than forty-two letters to secure *9d* a day for a clerk who had undergone a course of training in London and had taken to eating his luncheon in one of Lyons' tea shops. The Post Office opined that he had spent too much, that his subsistence allowance and out-of-pocket expenditure should have been ample, and should have produced some 'home saving'.

I produced the bills from Lyons' and insisted that the claim should be met, but some over-zealous chartered accountant at Headquarters went into research and hiding for a couple of months. When he emerged from his den his ten-page letter of reply carefully listed and compared Lyons' prices with those obtaining at the Central Telegraph Office refreshment club, subsidised by the Post Office. The claim was met after my short reply which informed the accountant that only members could use the CTO club, and that our trainee's application for membership was still under review.

Best bitter was *9d* a pint. It had taken three months to get those ninepences from the close fist of Headquarters, but we had a celebration at the Old Crown when the postal draft arrived.

My delight knew no bounds when I was elected conference delegate to Blackpool. The Post Office granted leave with full pay for 'Association Business' – which they later claimed from our union funds – and my out of pocket expenditure was met by the UPW. Before I left, the lads had a whip round to ensure that I did not fall into bankruptcy, and that was a moving experience. On the Saturday, complete with UPW badge, credentials, the motions of my branch, and stacks of coloured voting cards, I entrained with Dennis Wells, representing the Southall branch. No sooner had we taken a good meal in a comfortable hotel than we were shanghied and whisked to various secret meetings by the 'pressure groupers', those who wished to challenge and upset the plans of the

National Executive Council, and perhaps get elected to the 'top table' themselves before conference ended. They inspected our voting cards, to test our voting strength, and implored us to second their motions, to speak for them. In reply, they would do the same for ours. Democracy was at work!

Monday morning was an eye-opener. Conference was due to begin at 0900 hours. Dennis and I had not far to walk to that place of Lancastrian enjoyment where one Reginald Dixon used to rise from a well, seated on a stool, and play organ music for the BBC. We had our seating plans at the high port, badges in our lapels, folios in our hands, and the firm intention in our minds that we would be first in our seats – long before the multitude of over a thousand delegates. We could not have been more wrong. The minute we left our hotel we saw processions of brief-case carriers converging upon the Tower. There were wavings, shouted greetings, hand-shakings and a babel of all the dialects of the British Isles. A lump came to my throat. I belonged to something of importance. I felt like a Member of Parliament about to do great things for my constituency, even though it was a small-salaried sub-Post Office in industrialised Hayes.

At 0830 our credentials were inspected by a steward posted at the door, then we entered the large hall where the galleries were packed with people. On the floor, already three-parts filled, groups of men and women were in earnest conversation; others were waving to friends in distant seats, and the hall was pregnant with the chattering of happy people. Draped with flags and decorated with flowers the top table bulged with documents and bristled with microphones. Little groups of our national officers were behind that table, comparing notes, giving occasional waves to old colleagues. To the left and right of the top table were two rostrums, each with three steps leading to a microphone set on the lectern between two electric light bulbs. One light was amber, to encourage the speakers to speak up. The other red, to tell them to

1*a* Spike Mays, conference delegate

b Vera, John and Glyn, 1939

2a Sgt Mays, Royal Signals
Exercise Elephant, 1942

b Spike and Vera
de-mob suit, 1945

shut up. The first to speak was our Chairman. Smack on 0900 hours.

'I call conference to order.'

Conversation ceased. Paper rustlings and chair creakings took over for a few seconds before the Mayor of Blackpool entered with his crocodile of followers to give a speech of welcome. Hospitality to travellers was the ancient and virtuous theme of his erudition. Our attention was drawn to free facilities throughout our stay; buckshee squattings on beach and park deck-chairs; free swipes at golf balls on putting greens – on production of our trade union cards – and the free dance in the Tower Ball Room on Wednesday. Hope was expressed, but not too precisely, that we would spend all our pocket money in Blackpool. Following these preliminaries and the Chairman's address and annual reports, conference got into its stride, and from the floor delegates processed to the rostrum to do wordy battle against our employers, sometimes against the National Executive Council, but always for the lay membership of their branches.

This was my first experience of a public meeting of size. I was astounded and deeply impressed by the high standard of debate. Few of our officers and delegates had formal education, yet here they were speaking like professional orators and politicians, making me self-conscious and ashamed of my puerile prattle and limited vocabulary.

From the loudspeakers words cascaded in torrents, in varying degrees of vehemence and passion from Scottish throats; softer persuasions from the Irish, lilts and trills in Lydian measures from the Welsh, and voices in the dialects of most English counties. A confusion of accents rang in my ears long after I had gone to bed that night, for in my sleep the words were thundering in my brain. I wondered how such lowly people could rise to such linguistic heights. Dennis told me they were mostly self-taught; by reading, attending weekend schools and local debating societies, they had pulled themselves up the educational ladder by their Post Office bootlaces. I was determined to follow their example the moment I left Blackpool. More so after I had been introduced to some of our general officers. They were an erudite, dedicated and cheerful bunch, who took time to encourage fledglings like me.

Harry Wallace advised me not to lose a single opportunity to 'go back to school'. It was apparent that I needed educating. He was a classic example of 'do it yourself'. His education was elementary but he had been a member of the old Postmen's Federation and became the first Assistant Secretary of the UPW on its formation in 1920. From 1929 to 1931 he represented East Walthamstow in parliament (and was returned again in 1945), and served as Chairman of the Joint Industrial Workers. When I met him in 1937 he was an alderman of Lambeth Borough Council, and after the war he became a member of Lambeth Hospital Group Management Committee. He went with the parliamentary delegation to the United States, Berlin and Turkey, received the CBE in 1949, and became Mayor of Lambeth for 1952–3.

Harry Randall (The Quiff, we called him, because of his unruly blond hair – he looked much like Herbert Morrison) stalked around in full chatter like a perky cockatoo. Born in 1899, his education too was elementary; he became a member of the UPW as a postman in 1920, and was elected to the UPW Executive Committee in 1937. He was to become a most efficient Organising Secretary, and a delegate to the London District Council. He served on the Education Committee of the London County Council, was a governor of Ruskin College, Oxford, editor of the *London Post*, and extremely active in hospital work for the British Hospital Contributory Scheme Association. After the war Harry entered parliament as the member for Clitheroe (1945). He lost this seat in 1950 but was returned for Gateshead in 1955, when, because of a revision of UPW rules, he had to resign from the office of Organising Secretary. In the new parliament a motion was moved that no more M.Ps should hold office in the UPW. Harry served on many parliamentary committees and was British Delegate to the Council of Europe and the Western European Union in 1958–9.

Perhaps our best-loved Union M.P. was W. R. (Bill) Williams. Born at Cwmglo, a small mountain village in North Wales where his father was a quarryman, Bill progressed to Llanberis County School, and Caernarvon Grammar. Entering the Post Office as a paid learner in 1912, he was appointed to the Mold office in Flintshire, then served in the 1914–18 war, and afterwards transferred to Liverpool, where in 1929 he was appointed Central Secretary and Secretary of the Liverpool Whitley Committee. Bill was a devout Christian Socialist. He did not wear his religion as a badge to impress others, but embraced it as a light towards great truths. By those truths he lived. His deep lilting Welsh voice, his eloquence, good humour and gentleness were well known, particularly by the fine choir he led in the Sutton Welsh Chapel.

Bill's clear logical mind and an infinite capacity for work gained him a place in the Union's Executive Council, and in 1940 he was elected Assistant Secretary to represent the minor and manipulative grades (Indoor). In 1944 he was Chairman of the Departmental Whitley Council (staff side), and in 1945 he entered the House of Commons as Labour M.P. for Heston and Isleworth. Except for a short break in 1950–1, he served continuously in the House, for Droylsden, and later for Openshaw, Manchester, until the time of his death.

There is more to be said of Bill, for it was he who helped me to gain a scholarship and to go on to university. But two tributes in particular will not come amiss here. At the opening session of the 18th World Congress of the Postal, Telegraph and Telephone International in London on 16 September 1963, the month Bill died, President Carl Stenger referred to the great loss suffered by the PTT International and the British Post Office Unions by Bill's untimely death. A reference to his work for the Post Office was also made by the Postmaster-General, Reginald Bevins, who emphasised the respect in which Bill Williams was held by both sides of the House. Replying to those references, the Labour Party Leader Harold Wilson said this of my friend Bill:

> He was a big man in every way, whose devotion to the Union in which he had played so large a part, whose loyalty to the causes dear to his heart and, above all, whose integrity marked him out as a man all of us have been proud to know. He was our spokesman in the House on all matters affecting the Post Office. All people in the House – and none, I know, more than the Postmaster-General – are grieved by his passing.

His great friend Harry (The Quiff) Randall, with whom he served in the UPW and the House of Commons, paid this tribute:

> Bill Williams' life of selfless devotion is a challenge to each one of us. It was because he always had a great love in his heart for his fellow men and courage in his soul, daring to walk where men's tracks have not been implanted, that he made the rich discovery that striving for human happiness is worth the daily labour. Never did he shun the struggle – he faced it – for this was his gift and, together with his daily living creed, the driving force to his personal conduct and in his service for others.
>
> I mourn the loss of a dear friend. He was a good man who lived a good life.

I had not been long in Blackpool before I realised that the UPW was an ideal launching pad for parliamentary careers. Not that I had any personal ambition in that direction. In the cavalry I had heard magnificent officers describe such folk as third-class citizens only interested in getting 'M.P.' after their names, and whose sole object in life was to stir up international strife for soldiers to sort out. But I realised that the UPW provided opportunities for the development of other interests. Concerned about my further education, I had a word with one of the Union's stalwarts, who was to become its General Secretary and, eventually, a Life Peer.

Charles John Geddes, to us 'Charlie', now Lord Geddes of Epsom, advised me to attend evening classes with the local WEA, to apply to enter a technical college, and take a leaf out of his own 'do it yourself' book – one which now provides extremely interesting reading.

Born in 1897, he commenced his working life as a messenger in Peckham Sorting Office at the age of fourteen, became a telegraphist in the Central Telegraph Office, then served as a pilot in the Royal Flying Corps in 1914–18. He was Secretary of the Central Telegraph Office branch of the UPW in 1925, and was soon appointed Secretary of the Staff Side Whitley Committee. During this period he also served as branch delegate to the District Council, serving first on the Executive Committee before becoming Chairman of the full London District Council. By 1928 he had reached the Union's National Executive Council.

In 1937 he was Chairman of the Union, and in 1940 was appointed Assistant Secretary to the Staff Side of the Civil Service National Whitley Council. He resigned this post on being elected Assistant General Secretary of the UPW in 1940, and in 1944 became the Union's General Secretary. When he retired on 1 March 1957 we lost a good man.

The minute I learned in 1958 that Charlie had become a baron I sent him a message. 'Congratulations. We all knew you were worth your salt, but why choose Epsom?' The reply was appreciative, characteristically terse, but quite unprintable.

I have picked out these old friends of mine from many others of the same ilk not because they achieved the House of Commons or the House of Lords, but because in times far more difficult and frustrating than today they battled on with grim determination and made the Union of Post Office Workers the fine organisation it is. In addition to perseverance and dedication they possessed in good measure those valuable human qualities of humility, courtesy, tolerance and good humour. They all brought a bit of joy into the lives they touched. Their company was a pleasure, their conversation delightful and enlightening. Especially was it inspiring to see and hear them at the social gatherings each night after conferences. They would visit all 'the groups', as we called them, the contingents from Ireland, Scotland and Wales who used to herd in national pride in separate corners of the large bars. Charlie, Bill and the two Harrys would be there lifting up their voices in folk songs. Some bawdy, some not. The Welsh usually licked the lot, in volume and duration. But it always ended up in the same fashion. The choral groups would converge on to the Taffy gang, and by this time Bill Williams would be doing what he liked best of all, conducting. Leading all the 'foreigners' as they sang full-throat his favourite hymns and a psalm. We always started with 'The Lord is my Shepherd', to the melody of 'Crimond'. The Scots liked that one. For the English there would follow 'Abide with me'. The Irish loved that one. But we all loved the one that made Bill Williams close his eyes to hide the tears, usually the last, 'Jesu, lover of my soul', and we gave it justice, to the best of our ability and to the wonderful melody 'Aberystwyth'. It was good to see good men at work, and at play.

ELEVEN

Rise Soldiers, Rise

UNLIKE MY maternal grandfather Reuben Ford, I did not consider myself efficient, skilful and indispensable. Reuben was content with small mercies. He lived in the same hamlet cottage for over three-score years and ten; worked on the same farm for sixty years, produced thirteen children, food for them all and for many others besides; and apart from a broken leg which he set himself in the field and made a splint with a plough-spud to hobble home to Granny Ford, his only illness was his death. He had little regard for folk who talked unduly and did not work on the land. He lacked ambition.

'Where should any on us be if it worn't fer harvest?'

I had worked on the land for a time, and was glad to get off it. Like my grandfather, I had had no thought of ambition until I listened to the delegates of the UPW at my first Trade Union Conference in 1937. From then on I attended night classes of the WEA at Hounslow and Uxbridge, weekend schools of the UPW, and the Balham Drill Hall to train as a weekend warrior with the Supplementary Reserve.

These activities were over and above my forty-eight hour week at Hayes Post Office, when I mounted my red bicycle and made enquiries of Old Age Pensioners and others who had not paid their wireless licences. Some were enjoying radio silence. They could not afford new HT and LT and grid-bias batteries. I repaired broken-down wireless sets, dismantled outside aerials, and put lengths of phosphor-bronze wire under mats and over picture rails, before writing letters for them to the GPO to say they could not afford the licence fees. Those who could pay, but not Old Age Pensioners, I used to charge moderate fees which covered my fares to 'get-on-in-the-world' meeting places, and allowed me to buy books.

A kindly Ph.D. at Uxbridge lent me some books on Political Economy and Economics, and assured me that if I read, marked, learned and inwardly digested their contents I would one day gain a place at a university. The Education Branch of the UPW sent me pamphlets about postmasters and union officials past and present, the *Diaries of Beatrice Webb*, old copies of *The Post* (the journal of the UPW), tickets to attend ILP meetings at Seymour Hall, and gave me instruction and encouragement at weekend and summer schools. What with domestic decoration, gardening and odd spasms of boot and shoe repairing, life was hectic. I used to wind down on my trips to Balham Drill Hall, and there I discovered my heart was still very much in the army.

This came about by meeting ex-Lance Corporal 'Chesty' Wright, an ex-Royal Dragoon with whom I had served in England, Egypt and India. With ex-professionals from other units he had joined the Supplementary Reserve. We had little to learn about drill. Sometimes we were asked to train the rookies, but more often we were excused drill and went to have cooling pints in the canteen. We both missed the comradeship of the Royals, but one weekend were delighted when Sergeant Elkins commanded us – and two ex-professionals from an infantry regiment – to enter for the guard mounting competition. We all spat and polished a week in advance, just like old times. We each won a pewter pint pot – with plenty of useful liquid to put in it – and the competition. The GOC London District complimented us on our style and turnout. But the badge on the cup was not the Eagle of the Royal Dragoons, it was the Signals' badge, 'Jimmy on a rock cake'.

In the late spring of 1937 we went to camp for a fortnight, to spend most of our days learning teleprinter communication and line-laying, and most of our nights in local pubs – before returning merrily to camp to whip out the tent pegs holding up the canvas-clad messes of officers and senior NCOs. I earned a black mark and three extra drills. Chesty, who conceived the plot, was promoted to Lance-Corporal. I was ever accident-prone, but possessed what the newly-created military psychiatrists of the RAMC described as 'creative impulses', 'frustrated ambition' and 'a keen desire to succeed'.

I persisted with my studies at home for over a year. After my second UPW Conference in 1938 Harry (The Quiff) Randall gave me valuable assistance in recommending me for a scholarship to Ruskin College, Oxford, and I was due to attend that place of ivory towers in October 1939. In September 1939 the Supplementary Reserve was due for a fortnight's camp at Colwyn Bay. Both appointments had to be cancelled. Things were astir in the Polish Corridor. I found this out by accident.

One of the two Spratley brothers who kept a radio shop at Hayes had developed a yen to become a ham radio operator. I used to go round to his shop to train him in the Morse code. He could not get the PMG certificate and a licence to transmit until he could qualify in Morse sending and receiving at the minimal speed of twelve words a minute. Jack Witts, the Hayes Post Office overseer, sent me to Spratley's shop one morning to give him his final test; a certificate if he passed, the licence to transmit, and his own QSL (code) card. Spratley passed with honours. We whipped off our jackets, rolled up shirt-sleeves, put on the headphones and tuned the transmitter to our frequency on the ham band. A couple of flicks with Spratley's new high-speed, American 'bug' key, a glance at the output meter, and we realised we could speak to the universe on medium power, short-wave.

'Pick out a station, Spike,' said Spratley.

I selected a code name at random, called the station for about two minutes, then switched to 'receive'. We did a little dance of joy when our call-sign was repeated loud and clear without undue atmospheric interference. We made up odd messages, passing the time of day and other such pleasantries, then punched out at twenty words per minute that things were lovely in Hayes, and asked how were things in Warsaw?

Ear-shattering blasts in Morse almost fractured the diaphragms of our headphones when we switched to receive. Powerful instructions came from a monitor station, possibly the GPO or Military Intelligence. We were commanded to 'get off the air', but not before transmitting our QSL number, details of our transmitter, and our precise location. It transpired that we had been ether-chatting to an enthusiastic wireless ham who operated a military transmitter in the Polish Corridor. I have not clapped eyes on Spratley's set since that day, and only saw Spratley once, long after Hitler's war. Within a fortnight of our fraternising with the Poles I was called up.

It is not given to everyone to receive on his P.O. teleprinter an order to proceed to war. I did. The L. of C. Signals at Balham were more efficient than the police. They had lists of our offices as well as our home addresses. The instructions sent me were short and to the point.

REPORT BALHAM H.Q. 0900 HOURS FIELD SERVICE MARCHING ORDER.

I was annoyed, and thought of Rabbie Burns . . .

The best-laid schemes o' mice an' men
Gang aft agley,
An' lea'e us nought but grief an' pain,
For promis'd joy!

I cycled furiously to Hatton Cross, to my wife and two small sons. Vera was not amused. We telephoned, and made arrangements to store our furniture, to get Vera and the children off to

Wales, to her old home in Loughor, Glamorgan. Next day I reported to Balham for roll-call.

In the last week of August 1939 I oscillated between Balham H.Q. and my home at Hatton Cross, and was allowed to sleep at home. Days were spent in putting teleprinters and telegraph stores and equipment into huge packing cases for trans-shipment by air to France. Nights were more hectic, as Vera and I feverishly packed our belongings into tea-chests before her impending evacuation. On Friday 1 September, after handing our house keys to George Shankster next door, who had promised to get our furniture stored, I took Vera and our two boys to Paddington Station. Vera was bound for Wales, I for Wimbledon.

Paddington Station was chaotic. Droves of worried women and multitudes of children filled almost every inch of the station, waiting for the evacuation specials to take them to the safety of Wales. Platforms were filled to capacity and station staff were striving to keep the barriers closed. One woman committed suicide near a barrier; others were weeping and shrieking out the names of children who had been separated from them. I dumped our bags near a pillar, told Vera not to move from there, and went to buy tickets. When I returned Vera, the boys, our baggage and my kit-bag had disappeared. I tore down a couple of platforms and searched the length of two corridor-packed trains. There was not a sign of Vera. We had not said our farewells. I bounded the stairs to the Station Master's office and asked to use the announcement microphone. 'My bag must be in a train for Wales. In it are high priority military documents.' I was not allowed to use the mike, but Mrs Vera Mays's name was called, asking her not to proceed to Wales until I had seen her. I did not see her. She did not hear the announcement, the train had left. Soldiers had slung her in, with the boys, and with all the bags.

I caught the next train to Swansea and from there a bus to Loughor. Vera was at Tyrcoed, safe and sound with boys and bags, and had arrived only ten minutes before me. I stayed for a few hours then took myself and kit-bag to Wimbledon, where various plots were being hatched about the formation of Sections and Section Commanders. On Sunday 3 September, No. 48 Telegraph Operating Section had been brought up to War Establishment, and up some stairs to a flat-topped roof to hear the first wailing of London's sirens. We all looked skywards, and I could see the apprehension in the faces of our married lads. 'It can't last, it'll be over by Christmas!'

A few days later I reported to Heston Aerodrome with a dozen teleprinter operators from the Central Telegraph Office. All were expert telegraphists, some in Morse code, and were familiar with wireless communication. I was the only one from a provincial office. We were under the command of Captain Denman, a communications expert from the GPO. Twelve of us boarded a four-engined Albatross, while Dave Banham, six-foot three, with feet like pedestals, boarded a Dakota, together with the teleprinters and equipment of which he was placed in charge. His pilot was briefed to land at Folkestone to pick up a Verey Light pistol. Our pilot already had one.

Dave was the first of us to get a taste of war. For some reason unknown, his pilot did not land at Folkestone. When the Dakota was nearing the French coast it was buzzed by a couple of French fighter aircraft, the stumpy Blocs. They fired a few shells over and under the Dakota, to teach the pilot a lesson. The object of the Verey Light pistol was that it should be fired as an indication that we were friends. Dave quaked for days.

Due to some unprecedented oversight by the War Office we had the most comfortable billets in military history. We touched down at Le Bourget Airport where, for a few days, we took over the lounges and bars, and learned much about wine. Our mission was to strip the Paris Postale Télégraphe Téléphone of the old Baudot system of telegraphy – whereby persons perched on high stools operated a kind of piano keyboard, complete with black and white keys – and substitute our own teleprinters; 3As for tape and 7Bs for page printing; then demonstrate their use after our linesmen had connected them to the circuits. Frederick Court (Ding-Dong) Bell and two of his French-fluent friends from Faraday House (London's International Telephone Exchange) sat in with the pretty girls at the Paris exchange. If this was war, we could not get enough of it.

Mission accomplished in Paris, our reinforced L. of C. unit broke into smaller groups and repeated their educational performances in the larger garrison towns and seaports. Under Captain Denman's command twenty of us installed a signal office in the best lounge of the Hôtel du Casino, Cherbourg. We took over a nice house at 11 rue Noyon, where we lived in civilian style on superior rations. We brushed up our French, sunbathed on the beach and went on expeditions to the Maginot line to do repairs and install signals, but we always returned to Cherbourg. Apart from Ted Sleat who had served in the infantry, I was the only ex-professional soldier, but my colleagues were my seniors in territorial service, and lost no opportunity in reminding me of the circumstance. They behaved not in the least like soldiers of my day, but it was good fun. They played chess, the violin and piano, hockey and tennis. In the best *estaminets* of Cherbourg they herded to eat little chickens and sip dainty measures of wine before returning to 11 rue Noyon very early to write home – in duplicate, retaining the carbon copy. The only hazards they had encountered in their stool-polishing lives were contained between the stout covers of RG.17, the Staff Handbook of the GPO. Like true and faithful servants, which indeed they were, they continued to do what no war could stop them doing; to conform to the norm of the civil service. As companions they were hard to beat. As soldiers, but only at the beginning of their active service, they constituted the classic example of occupational maladjustment.

My suspicion that young Bill was a round peg in a square hole was confirmed the day I saw him attempting to remove the bolt from his Lee-Enfield rifle – with a hammer. Most of his training had been directed to the recognition of officers, rather than small arms and enemy aircraft, and Bill was the best saluter this side of Suez, a long-range saluter who detected and saluted officers almost out of sight. In his training no one had told him the function of the safety-catch. But for my intervention Bill's safety-catch might have remained at the 'on' position, and his bolt not withdrawn until V.E. Day. I explained and demonstrated. Bill was flabbergasted. Searching through his voluminous notes on how to become a warrior at weekends and finding nothing enlightening, he asked, 'Who told you? Have I missed a lecture?'

I confessed that in far-flung chunks of the British Empire I had fired 0.303s through Lee-Enfields, Hotchkiss, Vickers and Lewis machine-guns and other death-dealing devices.

'Coo!' said Bill. He hurried to tell Sergeant Bill Webber. Within minutes of his news seeping through the civil service crust I was promoted to lance-jack. Questions were fired at me from training pamphlets, of which we had a profusion. Like lightning I was put in charge of footdrill, weapon training and battery charging. Before I could bleat a syllable of protest Bill Webber asked me to solve a problem which had baffled the boffins for weeks . . . how to get the anti-tank rifle from its hermetically-sealed olive-green box. With the aid of a spade and a hammer I violated the box and disclosed one anti-tank rifle, two spare magazines, oil bottle and pull-through, and a most interesting leaflet which gave explicit instructions about how the box should be opened.

When battery charging was mentioned Balaclava flashed through my mind. I had stirring mental images of cavalry brigades charging 'sword-in-line' to winkle out disgusting gunners from cover. It transpired that the batteries were 12-volt DAG accumulators; secondary cells requiring primary charging and almost constant topping up with distilled water. Two Douglas petrol engines were also placed in my charge, together with one Freddy Gardener, an electrician. By this time I had deserted my digs in 11 rue Noyon and had a comfortable bedchamber in the Hôtel du Casino. But those petrol engines put a stop to that because I had to charge the batteries at night and snatch sleep in the daytime. Brigadier Beauman was to blame for losing me my room. He insisted on sleeping close to the signal office – in my room – and then complained that the racket from my engines disturbed his slumbers. Bill Webber commanded Lance-Corporal Mays and his pair of engines to remove to a place exposed to the elements – about four exhaust cable-lengths from the Briggy's boudoir. I gave the matter careful thought.

To remove a loose brick from the bottom course behind the wainscot of the Briggy's bedchamber was but the work of seconds. To wedge the business end of four exhaust cables joined in series into the hole was but the work of minutes. Within forty-eight hours our brigadier had gone up in the world; two floors, on Exercise Fume Dodge. Lance-Corporal Mays reoccupied the vacated premises. But there were drawbacks. From time to time, with contemptuous disregard for my privacy, inquisitive lieutenants of the English and French armies would burst into my room without knocking, mostly at highly inconvenient moments, and once when pretty Alice Lavalois the chambermaid was helping me with the bed linen. They always asked stupid questions about the location of unheard of admirals and field-marshals.

I noticed in the civil service army that the incidence of privacy disturbance always seemed to be in inverse ratio to rank and status. I also observed that apart from insignia of rank and superiority of cloth there was little discernible difference between the great-coats worn by officers and other ranks. After a bit of useful reconnaissance in the cloak-room I was able to attach brass crowns to the epaulettes of my great-coat each night before going to bed. With coat above the top blanket and crowns prominently displayed, my slumbers were less interrupted.

Life was quite luxurious. Each day I lunched with one of our two interpreters on the best fare of the hotel, either Sergeant Jacques Baume of the French Engineers (who stole the Town Major's bicycle and gave it to me under the eyes of the *gendarme* to whom he reported its loss), or Pierre Marchando, a handsome sailor Casanova from the Cherbourg Seaplane Base, who looked with lascivious longing at our red-caped ladies of the QAIMNS as they disembarked at the Gare Maritime.

'Just look at them, Spike, *mon vieux*! They are not made for war. For bed, yes . . . but for beds of love!'

Some evenings I dined with aged M. Picard, a French woollen manufacturer who gave me a magnificent long knitted scarf in black and emerald green for my wife. We used to play chess and drink Picon together until the pair of us could not see black from white, or tell rooks from pawns. We talked, but not of war. His subjects ranged from the works of Gabrielle Marcel, Rousseau and Jean-Paul Sartre to French brothels and English cigarettes; to all of which he was addicted.

Once in a while the boys congregated in the hotel lounge for sing-songs. As usual, we rolled out the barrel and hung out washing on the Siegfried line. One sing-song inspired the bard in Douglas Selway, a fine pianist who composed a song for 48 Telegraph Operating Section to the melody of 'Anchors a-Weigh':

When England's in a mess,
Just send for us.
We're the boys who'll pull her through,
And, if you don't believe it, try us.
Forty-eight are the best, of a bad lot.
But don't ask us to go to war, for
None of us can fire a bloody shot.

3*a* Bonnett Inn, Bartlow Hamlet

b Newbattle Abbey, Dalkeith

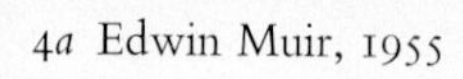

4*a* Edwin Muir, 1955

b Willa Muir, 1967

We had a major setback when the Cameronian Highlanders disembarked at the Gare Maritime. For several days they had been zig-zagging in the Channel dodging U-boats, but had only hard-tack haversack rations for one day, and almost undrinkable over-chlorinated water in their bottles. They were ravenous when they landed, and dry as brick-kilns. They invaded the hotels and *estaminets* to bolt down piles of eggs and chips, and drink bottles of wine like tots of ginger beer. Within two hours they were drink maddened, and took out their grievance on the town. So much so, that the town was put out of bounds to us all for some time, and we had to dodge the Red-caps by cunning. On our left arms we wore the blue-and-white Signals brassards, and were marched in correct formation to the various places of entertainment by senior NCOs.

Returning to the Hôtel du Casino late one night in the total blackout I heard a voice which brought back recollections of Aldershot in 1926 when I paraded for guard duty for the first time as a trooper in the Royal Dragoons and was picked for Stick Orderly for being the smartest man on parade. The inspecting officer was Lieutenant Roger Bright (Babe) Moseley. I felt sure it was his voice. It was certainly his style . . .

'Where the bloody hell is the Gare Maritime?'

'It is not far from here, Mr Moseley,' said I.

'Who the hell are you, and where are you?'

'Mays, once a Royal Dragoon.'

'Come here if you can find me.'

I found him, we shook hands in the blackout without seeing each other.

'You will be pleased to know that I have another Royal with me, Mays. Here is Colonel Hinton.'

I shook hands with Bill Hinton in the blackout. They were both colonels of a Yeomanry regiment. Bill had been Orderly Room Sergeant in Cairo. Shortly afterwards he was killed. I found that meeting a most moving and inspiring experience, and decided to mend my ways. The mood did not last long.

Active operations began in May 1940. From 16 May the German advance began to cut land lines and our teleprinter cables. Having seen the stout concrete protection of the Maginot line, and listened to the oft-repeated postulations of its inmates, '*Ils ne passeront pas*', we were astounded that the Germans had broken through.

From the beginning of the phoney war the French had never had much faith in wireless communication. On several occasions they had imposed long wireless silences, particularly with medium- and high-powered sets which they considered a security risk. Direction-finding sets could plot their precise locations and betray the whereabouts of GHQ. The result was that our wireless operators had little opportunity to exercise their skill and were unfamiliar with the new transmitters and receivers. But when the land lines were cut and the balanced cables of our intricate teleprinter system destroyed, there were frantic calls for a switch to wireless, and a kind of L. of C. witch-hunt to locate wireless operators.

In under twenty-four hours of the breakthrough, nine of us from 48 Teleprinter Operating Section who could punch Morse keys were ordered to fold up our tents in Cherbourg and glide through the night to Le Mans, to man wireless sets.

I was the only one who proceeded improperly dressed. My extensive touring of Manche on the Town Major's bicycle was to blame. Steel rat-trap pedals had played havoc with my ammunition boots, my only pair, whose soles had worn wafer thin. With part of my winnings at pontoon I attended Rattis' Selfridge-like store at Cherbourg and bought the only pair of boots that fitted me. They were brown, almost the same pattern as boots worn by officers. There were no more boots in our stores, and no military cobbler. So I took my worn boots to a French cobbler, who promised to repair them by next day. He did not, and when the call to arms came, I answered it in brown boots. My wireless operating colleagues had already left, so I proceeded alone. At Le Mans I reported to an office in the barracks, as ordered by my superiors. Apart from scores of pictures of naked French ladies on walls and lockers, the office was empty. Hungry and thirsty, deploring the loss of my bicycle, humiliated by having to travel dismounted, I washed, changed into a battle blouse without stripes, then flat-footed a mile into town to buy food and drink. Before I had marched forty paces I was saluted twice. Once by a sapper of the Royal Engineers, once by a Red-cap. With cavalry snap I returned both salutes, and then it dawned upon me . . . my brown boots! They thought I was an officer.

Through the basement window of a large building I could see masses of military persons working like beavers with maps, charts and cipher stencils. I tapped on windows, on doors; went through deaf and dumb motions to indicate that I wished to enter, to be accepted. No one paid the slightest attention. I moved off, hoping to find a café. Two down-at-heel Frenchmen accosted me. One asked if I had English cigarettes for sale. The other suggested that it might be to our mutual advantage if I went to bed with his sister, for a small fee. Then we were interrupted, and I heard the sweetest of music. A voice like a farrier's rasp rang out.

'Spike, you old bastard! What the hell are you doing here?'

Jigger Lee, originally in the Royal Corps of Signals at Catterick, had transferred to my regiment, the Royals, and we were together in Egypt in 1929, on the top rocks of Cheops, the biggest of the three shining lights of the East, the Great Pyramid. There we had stood to attention to drink a toast in chlorinated water from the River Nile, when I received a message by heliograph that King George V, our Colonel-in-Chief, had recovered from his penultimate illness. Next day I became sandblinded through reading the winks and blinks of heliographs over the blinding white sands and was admitted to the Citadel Military Hospital, Cairo. Before I emerged from that place, Jigger had been transferred again, to the 3rd Indian Divisional Signals, and I had met him again in Meerut.

It was like a breath of East Anglian spring to hear his voice. His face seemed more leathery than before – like the horse side of an unsoaped sweat-flap. We walked to a café, drew up chairs to a table and, stabbing skywards with two filthy fingers, Jigger hollered his order.

'Two bloody big beers!'

Two big Red-caps arrived as the beer was put down. Pipe-clayed from stem to stern, with Webley revolvers in their holsters and stupidity written on their faces, they gave us the once-over. Stretching a great paw in my direction, the taller barked at me, 'AB64!'

'It's at the barracks. I left it in my other battle blouse.'

'Why you wearin' brahn boots?'

I repeated the simple story, then the shorter one piped up.

'Meantersay you've come all the way from Cherbourg improperly dressed, wearin' officer's boots?'

'These are my boots,' I replied. 'I bought them at Cherbourg so that I would not be late for the real war, which I understand has just started.'

Jigger produced his pay book, handed it over and said, 'Know him well. He was in our old mob, the Royals.'

'What's your number then?' demanded the tall and ugly one as he closely examined Jigger's AB64.

'Three, nine, eight, five, three, seven! It's a cav. number, mate. Only six figures, an' it was dry before you were pupped.'

But in the book was written, 'four, three, seven', and Jigger had not noticed the clerk's inaccuracy. We were led off to the big house, put under lock and key and eyed with the greatest suspicion until the inquisition began. In about three hours, two hundred soldiers – or so it seemed – identified Jigger as their Section sergeant, and Jig was released, the only man in Le Mans who could vouch for my identity and patriotism. Slowly, the wheels of military intelligence began to grind. Security police were alerted. *Gendarmes* arrived with the two seedy Frenchmen who had spoken to me earlier. Telephone calls were made to Cherbourg, Dieppe and Paris. It was thought I was a spy.

'You were peering through windows and making signals in a highly suspicious manner. These Frenchmen were whispering to you.'

After explaining my footgear problem for the umpteenth time my identity was established by telephone from Le Mans Barracks. I was spared the firing squad, but because I had committed the heinous crime of buying brown boots I could not be let free.

'March him to the barracks,' said a staff captain to two Red-caps. 'Tell his C.O. to find him proper boots.'

Bill Webber met me, with crowns. He had been promoted to Sergeant-major.

'You will be confined to barracks until you get ammunition boots.'

'I shall not. Take me to the C.O.'

Smiles curled the major's lips as my tale unfolded, and he asked Bill for a pen.

'I shall write him a pass. We cannot confine one of our NCOs to barracks because he has bought boots to come to work with us, Sergeant-major!'

With Bill's pen he created a military precedent which was to disturb the sleep of military police in five countries, give nightmares to two civil service sergeant-majors, and cause two colonels to study the Manual of Military Law as it had never been studied before.

No. 398539 L/Cpl. C. W. Mays (2 L. of C. Signals)
is permitted to wear brown boots on all occasions.
J. Deakin, Major (Royal Signals)

There were no qualifying clauses, codicils, loopholes or legal booby traps. Major Deakin was good enough to be a cavalryman. Had he written 'on all fours' instead of 'on all occasions', I would have bought more boots to wear on my hands.

'I'm going into Le Mans,' said my new C.O. 'Hop in if you want a lift.' He allowed my former police escort to walk and dropped me at the café where Jigger had ordered the beers. My pass seemed to burn and vibrate in my battle-blouse pocket. It had been so gratifying to be saluted, to be taken for an officer. And it occurred to me that now I had authority to wear brown boots I should set my sights on pips and crowns. Go the whole hog and, maybe, get the King's Commission.

TWELVE

Retreat

For gold the merchant ploughs the main,
  The farmer ploughs the manor:
But glory is the sodger's prize,
  The sodger's wealth is honour;
The brave poor sodger ne'er despise,
  Nor count him as a stranger;
Remember he's his country's stay,
  In day and hour of danger . . .

Robert Burns

MAY 1940 turned out a hectic month of feverish searches for equipment, disruption of newly-formed wireless sections, the creation of others, and separation from friends. Before leaving Le Mans we opened all kinds of boxes and found enough radio equipment to fit out two 15 cwt trucks as mobile wireless stations. I had said goodbye to my friends of 48 TOS . . . Cecil Sugare, Monty Williams, John Trussler, Dave Banham, Alf Warne, Bill Webber, Doug Selway, and several others, before I was given maps and marching orders.

'Mays, you will go to Abbeville Aerodrome and maintain a constant listening watch until you receive further orders.'

Driver Gilbert, a Londoner who lived about eight inches from the Finchley Empire, and as good a comedian as any who had appeared on its programmes, drove us furiously to the aerodrome where French airmen, plus one Japanese pilot, were all dressed in flying kit ready to leap into their Bloc fighters. We parked our truck in the shade of a hangar, camouflaged it with nets and foliage, erected our aerial-pole with its umbrella-like spokes, then reported to a young lieutenant of the Royal Signals. We were not enthused by his welcoming speech.

'You man the set, Mays. Keep your ears and eyes open. We are expecting to be bombed any minute.'

We had only ten minutes to wait. It was a lovely May morning. The sun was giving its best in a bright blue sky stippled and mottled with cotton-wool puffs of clouds. The red-tiled roofs of the town poked prettily and peacefully through surrounding trees; and in the fields old men in striped shirts were hoeing long rows of plants that were unfamiliar to me.

We heard them before we saw them; three bombers double-droned then dived above the red roofs and released their bombs. Three squat Bloc fighters roared into the sky from behind us and gave chase. Only two returned, but one bomber was brought down. We watched it crash into the trees.

'Thank Christ!' yelled Gilbert. 'They've got one of the bastards.'

Within one hour we had two lots of visitors. The first was a French pilot on a haywain, his head so bullet-riddled that it looked like a mop of blood. They carried him to the medical wing on an old hurdle. The French guard presented arms.

An ambulance came. Inside it were three Germans, all young, sunburnt and flaxen-haired. Two were taken to the guard room, and were spat upon by the guard. The third, the tail-gunner, had a white flying suit. When they lifted him blood spurted from bullet holes, reminding me of old Granny Ford straining elderberries in her colander. This was my first bit of Hitler's war, but before I could philosophise the Messerschmidts were on us. Shells churned up grass and tarmac, flame and smoke billowed, the old truck rocked and was splintered and our aerial rod received a knock which bent it into a question mark. Driver Gilbert did not seem at all put out . . .

'Look at the bleedin' aerial, Corp. If you call Control you'll be sendin' twisted signals!'

Pale and scared-looking, our young subaltern was competent and brave. 'Is the set all right, Mays? Have you a fag?' He drew in the smoke in a long, hard pull which burned the paper almost half-way down the cigarette; otherwise he was rock steady.

'The set's all right. How about you?'

'I am bloody-well annoyed. We've done nothing in return, and there is this awful feeling of helplessness. That's all!'

French mechanics helped us with repairs before bringing us liberal tots of Calvados which burnt our throats and cheered us. We remained at Abbeville for a few days, maintaining a twenty-four hour listening watch and hearing instructions being given to various units of 3rd Division. Some had to fall back on Furnes, others on Nieuport, under the command of Montgomery. GHQ was on its way to La Panne under Lord Gort. What peeved us most was the instruction that the whole of the BEF was to be put on half rations because supplies had broken down and the food situation was becoming desperate. Local commanders were left to use their own initiative and make their own decisions about movements. We received instructions to move to a small farm in the village of Le Pin where there was a battery of light ack-ack. We stayed there three days; were ordered to refrain from smoking – even in clear daylight – and to adopt the prone position in the woodlands and speak only in whispers. Each day we heard the drone of enemy bombers overhead, but not a shot was fired. One morning all hell broke loose, our ack-ack was in action. The target was a Dakota, barely above tree height. Its British markings and registration number could be read with the naked eye, but not for long because they shot it down. The plane landed in a field about 300 yards from the farm. Sentries were posted round it, but only to stop us going along to look for letters from loved ones. For its passenger load the Dakota had several VIPs from British and French Post Offices. For freight, hundreds of bags of mail. Letters littered adjacent fields, and our lads were far more annoyed about that than by having to stop smoking.

We were then ordered to Lisieux to pick up petrol. We did not realise at the time that the petrol was to take us to Dunkirk, but it was really a miracle that we managed to negotiate the Paris–Lisieux Road. Packed solid with refugees who trundled hand-carts, bicycles and even children's toy trolleys laden with worldly possessions, it was difficult to move more than a couple of miles an hour along that road of human misery. When the refugees were not imploring us to give them our hard-tack biscuits and water – for there was neither bread, wine, nor cider to be had at that time – they would be looking skywards, in fear of the next hail of shells from Heinkels and Messerschmidts. For a few months I had a souvenir of that barbarity, a little silver medallion of St Christopher, given to me by a dying French nun. She had been carrying a small child whose mother had been killed earlier that day. I gave her water and bits of biscuits. Her feet were torn to shreds and she lay in a pool of blood. I bandaged her with my field dressing. She gave me the medallion, then died.

Vast pyramids of petrol cans were piled at Lisieux. They had been there a long time. So long that petrol trickled from rust-eaten corners of the two-gallon cans, and poured from the perforations in others. We filled our jerry-cans, then made up a couple of truck-loads from tins that were not leaking. But before we moved off I noticed petrol leaking to the truck floor, and told Gilbert about it.

'I'll drive that bleeder,' said Gilbert. 'You drive behind in the wireless truck, an' keep yer mincers open. If it sets fire give us a toot an' I'll nip aht. Right?'

I explained that if it set light he would set light with it.

'Belt up! Some silly bastard's gotta do it. Might as well be me!'

We drove to the rendezvous and delivered the petrol without trouble, and then were shuttle-cocked by radio instructions and six-figure map references along second- and third-class roads less refugee-packed; but we were too late for the Dunkirk evacuation. It was all over. Montgomery had got away, and most of his men, thank heaven, before we were near the place.

For a couple of weeks we groped our way towards Cherbourg with Brigadier Beauman, and two escorting tanks that impeded our progress. One had shed a main track pin. To retain it as an escort we had to move forward about five kilometres; strip the sound tank of a pin, then ferry it back to the faulty one. We kept up this leap-frogging business far too long, but eventually the tanks were disabled and we proceeded without them. Just before entering Cherbourg we saw the English Channel from the top of the Montagne du Roule, and were quite chirpy about the sight. But the Luftwaffe had seen us. For most of the time since Dunkirk we skulked in hedges, ditches and copses by day, and had moved only at night, but it was early morning when we neared Cherbourg. Two Heinkels swooped on us and ripped holes through our floorboards, fortunately without hitting us. Possibly because they had run out of ammunition, they did not give us a second helping. We hid again, then made for St Nazaire where, after chopping up wireless sets with axes and blowing up our trucks, we boarded a boat and set sail for Blighty – almost three weeks after Dunkirk.

My strongest recollections of the trip across the Channel are the two stories we were told almost as soon as we pulled out of the port. One concerned a young officer who when boarding had been asked in the interests of safety to ensure that the anti-tank rifle he carried was not loaded. To find out he pressed the trigger. A 0·505 bullet perforated two soldiers – life jackets and all – and both were killed and buried at sea. The other concerned the disaster which had befallen the *Lancastria* not long before. Just before she was about to up-anchor at St Nazaire a bomb was dropped down a funnel. Over 2,000 soldiers died. I felt pleased to be alive and went to sleep on the upper deck. We had not enjoyed much sleep from the middle of May. When I became fully restored to consciousness, after landing and struggling about in the dark, I regretted the circumstance. After an awful breakfast I found myself on that lousy chalk in abominable Blandford Camp, Dorset. There were compensations. Quite a number of my friends from 48 TOS were present, but we did not stay there long. One morning shrill whistle blasts called us out on to the chalk where we received instructions.

'Get dressed in FSMO. We move off in half an hour!'

Before that day's light had fully waned our train pulled up at a small Yorkshire station. We had arrived at Knaresborough. In the Town Hall there was spread a feast – to welcome us as heroes. Complete with speeches from Town Councillors, good food, pints of beer, invitations to further meals and beds in the homes of the inhabitants of Knaresborough and Harrogate, and offers from many willing helpers to put down beds for us on the Town Hall floor, it was most moving, if totally unjustified appreciation. Unprecedented kindness and hospitality were showered on us. We were made honorary members of various clubs. Not a social, sex or political barrier was put in our way. We had only to ask, and we would have become life members of the Women's Institute and the Mothers' Union.

At that time walls were suspected of sprouting ears, and because troop movements were the common currency of civilian conversation, we were given but a hint of our next destination. A musical comedy version of a military staff captain complete with the upper-lip bushgrowth of some RAF types tried to warn us to be cautious.

'You'll be leaving Knaresborough pretty soon. Can't say where you're bound, chaps, but here's a clue . . . I hope you like whisky and porridge!'

Forty-eight hours later, just as dawn was breaking, we staggered fully-laden up steep steps leading from Edinburgh's Waverley Station. Between the tramlines of Princes Street we fell in for roll-call, then turned left and marched down Europe's best thoroughfare, under the shadow of Auld Reekie's historic castle, to take over St George's School, Roseburn.

THIRTEEN

Auld Reekie

When wild war's deadly blast was blawn,
   And gentle peace returning,
Wi' mony a sweet babe fatherless,
   And mony a widow mourning;
I left the lines and tented field,
   Where lang I'd been a lodger;
My humble knapsack a' my wealth
   A poor but honest sodger.

Robert Burns

TO THE EAST of Corstorphine Hill, the Scottish Zoological Park and golf course, and standing on high ground north of Murrayfield, St George's School is a most imposing building surrounded by well-kept gardens and playing fields. Gentle Scottish ladies had been taught there before we ravished its woodwork, and began to get into our stride to take revenge upon the Wehrmacht. We did not get off to a good start. In periods of uncertainty the army relies upon drill, especially in the practice of marking time. Scottish Command was no exception. When not engaged in crushing the turf of playing fields at footdrill, we saluted. There were lots of officers to be saluted in Edinburgh at the time. Next, we attended to our somewhat slovenly appearance. New battledresses were issued from the stores, enough to make Auld Reekie reek of camphor. We took our new suits to Forsyths, the expert tailors just off St Andrew's Square, to get lily-white stripes, the insignia of Scottish Command for shoulder tabs, and virginal medal ribbons. We ordered the Royal Signals blue and gold dress forage caps, to wear with our tailored blouses on our perambulations up and down Princes Street and along the walks and paths of its lovely gardens. There was method in this madness. Edinburgh bristled with sailors, soldiers and airmen of other nations. Our Allies were sartorially splendid. Their turn-out gave them an edge over us with the lassies.

There were clusterings of Czechs, profusions of Poles, flotillas of Frenchmen and, last but not least, swarms of kilted and sporraned Scots. Apart from the disadvantages of inferior dress, first and foremost, we did not know the language. Poles with Polish–English dictionaries paraded at tobacco kiosks to chat to sales girls. Czechs played chess with curvaceous college girls. French sailors everywhere held hands with the lassies.

There were no English–Scottish dictionaries, but there were stories going round about the language problem. One concerned two lassies from Glasgow who stopped at a Rose Street greengrocery and delivered a lesson to their escorts, two splendid Polish officers of cavalry mien, encrusted with patent leather, brass and braid and the manners of diplomats.

'Uf yew yins'll lear-r-n us yins tae talk Pollish, us yins'll lear-r-n yew yins tae talk Unglish.' One girl pointed to the stall. 'Them's apels, them's ingins, an' them's tatties (apples, onions and potatoes).'

The English wife of an officer just posted to Edinburgh was soon put in her place by a butcher . . .

'I want to buy a sheep's head to make the Majah some brorth, my man!'

Tam called to his assistant, 'Wullie . . . ship's heid!'

Willie brought in a newspaper-wrapped parcel. Disdainfully, the lady poked it with the ferrule of her brolly and asked for it to be unwrapped, adding, 'Is it an English sheep's head?'

'Och, noo! It's Scottish.'

'But I particularly want an English one.'

'Wullie! Tak' it back. Scrap oot the brain. Put in anither tongue!'

But we settled down and for several months enjoyed the lavish hospitality of the Edinburgh Scots, who took us to their hearts and homes, to theatres, film shows, and concerts rendered by Polish choirs in the Usher Hall. 'Married crocks' sent for wives and children. Vera came with John, but left Glyn aged two in Wales. They arrived in time to hear the first German bomb hit a whisky distillery, and stayed in a Roseburn flat with charming Mrs Brown. In no time at all John developed an Edinburgh accent and insisted on 'chumming' people home. We spent weekends on voyages of discovery in the beautiful environs of the city, and 1940 passed pleasantly and reasonably peacefully. Vera and John returned to Wales.

New equipment then arrived and training was intensified. Two officers were largely responsible, Major H. V. G. Bloodworth (who was to become the British army's youngest brigadier), and a Scottish lieutenant with a strange name, Bujnowski. We called him 'Budgie'. They quickly put a halt to footdrill and saluting by making practical preparations for D-Day. Wireless schemes were the order of the day in the Lowlands and Highlands, with spells of Commando training in the Cairngorms and the climbing of Ben MacDhui. Teleprinter operators were trained in Morse and wireless and taught the tricks of light automatic arms, the Bren and the Sten, and to drive all M.T. vehicles in our charge – for which they were issued with driving licences from St Andrew's House. We took pride in learning these new skills, after the Dunkirk *débâcle*. I qualified as a radio mechanic and was promoted to Corporal.

In the late evening of 3 May 1941 I returned to St George's School and found a telegram on my bed.

COME CEDRIC OUR GLYN IS DEAD.

I applied for compassionate leave. Train services were chaotic with poor connections and long waits, but I arrived at Tyrcoed where Vera was prostrate with grief. Just over two and three-quarter years of age, our little son looked like a wax doll. In his hand was a narcissus, his favourite flower. On his face that questioning smile that will forever haunt us. Those Loughor people were so kind, so understanding. Only the menfolk attended the funeral, as is the custom in Wales. I walked in battledress with a black armband at the head of a long procession of mourners from Tyrcoed to Moriah Chapel, where Glyn was placed in the Jones family grave. For my benefit the Reverend John William Lunt conducted a most moving service in English. He touched on the stupidities of war and the disruption of family life. His words helped to soften the bitter blow, and I sometimes sense his comforting arms round my shoulder and feel again the grasp of his hand. Vera was inconsolable. I telegraphed to Edinburgh . . .

WIFE GRIEF STRICKEN UNSAFE TO LEAVE REQUEST LEAVE EXTENSION TO 14TH.

The reply came in the afternoon.

EXTENSION GRANTED TO 24TH.

But on the 16th a policeman of the Glamorgan force came to tell me that I had overstayed my leave and had better get back. I produced the telegram.

'Hang on then, boy. You've got another eight days. I'll telephone.'

Two days later two military policemen arrived from Swansea. They snooped round to the back door, peered in without knocking, and my father-in-law took them severely to task.

'We don't have police spies round our back doors. Go to the front. Knock on the door like gentlemen, and behave.'

I showed them the telegram. They were surprised, but kind.

'There must be some mistake. Your RSM told us on the phone that your leave had been extended to the 14th. Don't go back until tomorrow. We'll ring and explain.'

I had to appear before my C.O. on my return. Checks were made at the Edinburgh Post Office. A teleprinter operator had typed '2' instead of '1'. I was very relieved to learn that no one got into trouble about the mistake, and I telegraphed Vera to put her at ease. It transpired that our Glyn had been ill for a month with a cerebral infection. Vera had not told me. She did not wish me to worry. One night he slipped quietly away in his sleep, and I was not there to comfort her.

One morning Major Bloodworth sent for me.

'Mays, I have a job for you. How would you like to become the wireless instructor for a squadron of GHQ Liaison Regiment? You may have seen some of them. They wear a white letter "P" on a black shoulder-tab and are known as the Phantoms. Their function is communication, to transmit information from forward areas direct to GHQ without going through the normal communication channels of the Signals. They have fast armoured cars, machine-guns and medium-power wireless sets and they work in troops and squadrons. What do you think about it?'

'When can I start, sir?'

'Good! You will start tomorrow, and will be made sergeant from today. There will be plenty for you to do. Good luck. We shall need efficient operators before we are very much older.'

Within two days I left Edinburgh, bound for Richmond, Surrey. I reported to an hotel almost opposite the Star and Garter Home for Disabled Soldiers and was ordered to attend a meeting then in progress. There was a sprinkling of NCOs and many officers, who seemed to represent most of the standing army of Britain. One wore the badge of the Rifle Brigade, and seemed vaguely familiar to me. And then I remembered

I had seen him on the silver screen, putting armlocks on Claudette Colbert. It was David Niven.

The adjutant put me in the picture:

'We are forming another Squadron for the Scottish Command. Your commanding officer will be Major Mervyn Vernon of the Grenadier Guards. You will return to Edinburgh tomorrow and bring down the new squadron for training. It will be called E Squadron, and you will be its wireless instructor. You will continue to wear your Signals badges, but you will wear the Phantoms shoulder-tab.'

I was handed fifteen rail warrants made out to Richmond from Edinburgh, and another for myself to proceed and return. I reported to Major Vernon at No. 9 Spylaw Road, Edinburgh, a place not far from an asylum. There I assembled my trainees; cooks, butchers, carpenters, machine-gunners, one pioneer and one officer's servant. There was not a regimental signaller in the batch. None appeared to have heard of the Morse code, so I knew a busy time lay ahead of me.

On my second meeting with Major Vernon I put a foot wrong by asking why I should take fifteen men to Richmond for what appeared to be nothing more important than a roll-call, before bringing them back again to Edinburgh for training. I was soon put in my place.

'You were a professional soldier and should know better. Your job is to obey orders. Understood?'

'Sir!'

He had brought two sergeants of the Grenadier Guards, Les Cullen and Sandy Powell, from his own battalion to take care of questions, drill and discipline. I asked no more questions. Before many weeks had passed our odd assortment of military tradesmen began to behave like soldiers of the Brigade of Guards. They crashed down their feet like steam hammers, saluted everything that moved and blancoed everything static. More important as far as I was concerned, they learned Morse quicker than their commissioned superiors and took a keen interest in mastering the technique of radio communication. I fitted up two large tables with headphones and Morse keys, and sent cipher groups and plain language messages to officers and men for an hour or two each day. One morning, after I had been sending to one of the classes, Major Vernon appeared and asked a young subaltern to read out what he had received.

'I am improving,' said the subaltern, 'I have read three Es.' Major Vernon was not impressed, and rightly so, the letter E in Morse being just one dot – and I had been keying away for nigh on twenty minutes.

'What is your difficulty? You must do better than this.'

'There is only one thing which prevents me reading Morse better than Sergeant Mays,' replied his nibs. 'It is my total incapacity to distinguish dots from dashes.'

We continued training throughout the summer, touring Scotland and setting up troop radio stations at remote points. One exercise lasted almost a month with educational halts at Inverness, Golspie, Dornoch, Brora, and many places in between, before we moved on a long trek to Wick and Caithness then west to Ullapool before returning to Edinburgh. It was a most memorable and enjoyable trip. The sun shone hotly most of the time and when we removed our chin-straps there were white lines on our faces like tribal marks.

I had one fault to find with this first-class unit and tried to set it right. For all-important communications from the forward battle areas to GHQ the messages were sent in a phrase code of four-letter words. For example the word 'GOON' might represent a whole sentence, such as 'Return to H.Q.' I considered this code far too distinctive, for no other communication unit used anything like it. It occurred to me that once enemy listeners heard the code they would be able to identify us and, with the aid of their D-F equipment and radio compasses, draw the attention of their artillery and air forces to our exact location. I mentioned this to our Signals Officer, but he was not impressed at the time. One day, by sheer accident, I was able to prove I was right. After putting in new electrolytic condensers to a faulty set I spun the tuning dial of the receiver and listened to signals throughout the frequency range. To my surprise I heard a group of stations using our phrase code, and I reported to Major Vernon who ordered me to take down every dot and dash.

'It cannot be anyone in England or Scotland, Mays. None of our squadrons is operating.'

De-coding of the messages revealed that one of our squadrons was operating, but in Ireland, on the Mountains of Mourne.

'If you can hear them, they should be able to hear us, Mays. Can you chip in and upset the blighters?'

'If they hear me I can take over control of the group, with your permission, sir.'

'Good! Get mobile!'

One by one the four troops of the squadron replied to my signals. I then sent a coded message to the control station that I was assuming control, and reported their acknowledgement to Major Vernon.

'Well done, Mays! Send the blighters this message.'

The message was simple, if unmilitary . . . 'Love and kisses, Hitler.'

'Send them another. Tell them to get off the air and return to base.'

All four troops and the control station of the squadron in Ireland ceased communication and returned to their H.Q., much to the consternation of an irate brigadier who had been flown from London to witness and report upon the exercise. Having scoured the Mountains of Mourne in vain, he reported his non-findings to London and there was hell to pay. At a special meeting of the top brass of Intelligence at Scottish Command Headquarters, Major Vernon and I were taken to task for 'extraordinary behaviour', but explanations were made and the heat died down.

A somewhat similar, but tragic incident occurred in February 1942. I had spun the receiver dial of a No. 9 set to an American station using automatic Morse at about 25 words a minute. I wrote the whole of the transmission on the back of message pads. It was a distressing bit of news which did not appear in the press for a long time afterwards. It told of the Japanese air attack on the city of Singapore; the capture of the water supplies; the total destruction of the military bases and the surrender of 70,000 men.

I telephoned Major Vernon at his office on the far side of Spylaw Road and asked to see him. He was most distressed when he read the news.

'Have you mentioned this to anyone?'

'No, sir!'

'Good. Don't breathe a word to a soul.'

And I did not, until now.

But I never discovered whether our phrase code was discontinued. Shortly afterwards I had to say goodbye to the Phantoms, albeit with great reluctance. My friends had all gone from St George's School to North Africa. It appeared that 2 L. of C. Signals had ceased to exist. I was called to Scottish Command Signals at Redford Barracks, Colinton, Edinburgh, to work on high-power radio from concrete bunkers near Juniper Green. I discovered that my new C.O. and Major Bloodworth had given me first-class recommendations and certified that I was technically qualified to hold commissioned rank in the Royal Signals. The news had leaked, and to my delight I received a most kindly letter from the Phantoms.

E Squadron
GHQ Liaison Regiment
5-7-1942

Dear Mays,

I am very sorry that I was not able to say goodbye. We are all very sorry that you have left us and thank you for training our squadron to such a high state of efficiency.

You should be able to get your commission without a lot of rope-climbing nonsense; and if there is anything Major Vernon or any of us can do to help, don't hesitate to let us know.

Best wishes,
R. L. Stileman.

I still had my brown boots and the pass permitting me to wear them, and now, this letter. All I had to do was to await instructions to attend the next War Office Selection Board. I could almost smell the pips.

At 0815 hours on a Monday in 1942, Phillips yelled to me from our gin palace (15 cwt radio truck). We were camping at the foot of the Pentland Hills, midway between Currie and Balerno.

'Spike, H.Q. want you. Bet it's about Benford!'

I took the microphone and spoke to Sgt (Blanco) White, and was relieved to learn it was not bad news about Benford, who, without eyelashes, eyebrows or hair of head, was in the Military Hospital – on account of our cess-pit getting smelly and wee-beastie ridden. Without disinfectant, Benford had tried to disinfect it by pouring into the hole one jerry-can of W.D. petrol. He threw in a lighted match. Nothing happened. Being of a naturally inquisitive disposition he peered into the hole just as the volcano erupted. The CSM was enraged, and we now awaited a Court of Enquiry. Blanco's news was a tonic . . .

'Get cracking. You're s'posed to be at "Wosby" (War Office Selection Board) at ten o'clock, mate. But they've only found the letter just now, in the wrong tray. Take the gin palace!'

I hurled myself into the truck, drove furiously to Redford Barracks, changed into my best battledress and drove to a stately Scottish mansion to the east of the Pentland Bounds. I was ten minutes late, but the circus had not begun. A staff captain ushered me into the drawing room where deep armchairs held ill-at-ease candidates for commissioned rank. Some were pretending to read the *Economist*, *The Times*, the *Scotsman* and other socially esteemed literature. Others were watching and taking copious notes, which reminded me of certain tips given to me by Tam Sutherland.

'Keep a sharp look-out. Half will be War Office wallahs disguised as soldiers to spy on you. They'll watch you eating, listen to your yap and such to see if you were dragged up right. If you're not public school, you've had it, cock!'

After coffee and biscuits an expert arrived.

'Good morning, gentlemen! Tomorrow we shall begin to sort the wheat from the chaff. First, there will be gymnastics and tactical exercises. These have been designed to test your physical fitness, your agility, and so on. Next day you will have verbal and writing tests. Nothing to worry about, school children pass them with ease. If you survive, and I am sure that you will, you will be passed to some of our staff officers who will question you on current affairs and your personal history. You know the form; general knowledge, a bit of history and geography; that sort of thing. Afterwards, you will see the psychiatrist. No need for alarm. We don't suspect you of being round the bend. He will ask special questions. From your answers and the previous results, he will be able to determine whether you are introverted or extroverted. Sounds frightening, but there's nothing to worry about. We are out to discover if you have manipulative or verbal skills. We need the 'manips' for the scientific weapons of modern warfare; the 'verbals' for Admin. and Intelligence. Good hunting, and the best of luck to you all!'

The day passed pleasantly. Lunch was nothing to write home about. At my place, where I expected to see battalions of knives, forks and spoons – and possibly a finger bowl – I found one bluntish knife, a sulphated dented fork, two spoons and a paper napkin. The soup was brown, possibly from Windsor. The main course, fish and chips, was on the tepid side, but the coffee, cheese and biscuits were most enjoyable. My fellow diners chatted throughout. Some feigned the speech mannerisms of the *élite*. All but one professed to know someone of enviable social status. He was an old soldier, a private from the Gordon Highlanders who, unlike the remainder and the frog of Confucius fame, opened his mouth only to eat.

Next morning we paraded in the gymnasium where we climbed up specified ropes and slithered down unspecified ones. There was some profound psychological significance about the ropes we selected for descent. We did handstands, short-arm balancing, hurled ourselves up wall-bars and over horses. I enjoyed myself getting in a couple of good punches to the midriffs of two CSMs in a free-for-all rugger wall game. All the time we were under the eyes of the experts, who wrote things about us in books. Feverish excitement prevailed in one corner of the gymnasium where stood a mammoth skittle board with monster skittles arranged upon it in a certain order. The object of this exercise was to rearrange the skittles in the minimal time and to eliminate superfluous movements. I believe the excitement was generated because the experts had made bets.

After lunch we dressed in FSMO and sallied forth to the Pentland Hills to outwit plots to booby-trap us in ditches and copses. Having erected improvised bridges from railway sleepers which miraculously appeared where trains had never passed, we were ordered to race hot-foot back to the stately mansion; to test our speed for retreat and our homing instinct.

Next morning I opened the folder of Test Paper 1, and disclosed a Projective Technique Test designed by psychologist Rorschach. Odd-looking cards bore odder-looking ink blots, and an instruction.

LOOK AT EACH CARD. WRITE EVERYTHING YOU SEE ON EACH CARD AS YOU LOOK AT IT.

Because not a word appeared that this test had been designed to test our personalities, and because I suspected some kind of trap, I wrote 'Blots'. Next came the TAT (Thermatic Apperception Test), in the form of a series of harrowing photographs. Negro gentlemen with scared faces were climbing up or down long ropes. Old ladies clad in shawls – their faces contorted with anguish – were weeping and stretching out imploring hands. Little boys in velvet suits and lacy Peter Pan collars were looking in pleasure or pain at broken violins. There were others which I am glad to have forgotten; not one seemed to have the remotest relationship to soldiering. But there was an instruction:

WRITE A STORY ON EACH. YOU HAVE LOTS OF TIME. DON'T HURRY.

I have forgotten what I wrote. It was never published.

Then followed the I.Q. test, one of many designed by Francis Binet. There were whirls and whorls, dots and triangles, circles and rectangles and strange smudges. From these we had to make our patterns. Then came progression problems on geometric and arithmetic ratio that would have put Einstein and Bertrand Russell in the luny bin. But the most cunning and significant of all the tests were contained in the seemingly harmless questionnaire.

What school did you go to?

What was your father's occupation?

*Do you consider that saluting should be maintained during war?

*Do you consider that social distinction should be maintained during war?

*(If you have strong views on these subjects indicate by placing X in the margin.)

I put an X against each, but knew I would live to regret it.

'Enlightening' would be the best description of the inquisition by several staff officers. They did not waste a lot of time.

'You were a professional soldier, in the Royal Dragoons?'

'Sir!'

'But you have strong views about saluting. Let me hear them.'

'I have done a lot of saluting and consider that it serves no useful purpose except making the saluted feel important. I was taught that I was saluting the King's Commission, not the man. But it is the men who get annoyed, not the monarch, when salutes are not given.'

'Very interesting. Anything else?'

With due humility I suggested that perhaps too much time had been devoted to saluting but not enough to weapon training; quoting the case of young Bill who, after only six months' training was the world's best saluter, but had been unable to extract the bolt from a Lee-Enfield. There was a great huddling of red-capped heads whose faces frowned. Next morning I was hustled to the psychiatrist, a shrunken being bearing major's crowns and the serpentry insignia of the Royal Army Medical Corps (Rob all my comrades). His welcome was a ferocious look and two minutes' silence as he read the reports on my file. The silence was broken by his posing peculiar questions. The army, it appeared, was most concerned to know if I had wet my bed in infancy and in adolescence, and if I loved my mother more than my father and if I was an only child.

He glared at my feet. 'You shoe-lace is undone!' I did not look down. The boys had told me about this one; but I reminded him that I was wearing ammunition boots, not shoes; that when I laced them in cavalry style they stayed laced – all day. He wrote things on my psychograph. The interview was over. I saluted, marched to the door and looked back as I closed it. The wizard was yawning.

My bitterest disappointment was that I had let Major Bloodworth down. I had been a professional soldier for twelve years and served at home and abroad and had been selected to train commissioned ranks. As Tam Sutherland had forecast, the ex-school teachers and previous inmates of public schools were accepted. They, presumably, were the 'verbals', for they could not slope arms. I was very upset, and was again reminded of that hymn we had to sing to the parson in my village school:

The rich man in his castle, the poor man at his gate;
God made them high or lowly, and ordered their estate.

FOURTEEN

Mount and March

ALTHOUGH I had a great love for Edinburgh's beauty and distractions I could not put from my mind my failure to pass the WOSB. There were so many officers. All had to be saluted. Each of my salutes was a reminder of stupidity. I applied to be posted to North Africa, perhaps to meet up with some of my old friends from 2 L. of C. Instead of sunny Africa I was bundled off to a Holding Unit on Thirsk Race Course – to sleep in the open and to find each morning that my coir-packed bolster had been frost-welded to stiff spikes of white-rimed grass. After a month of inferior food, chaotic administration and nightly refrigeration I was glad to be posted to St John's Wood Barracks, NW8. There for three nights I found a frost-free corner bed space. On the fourth morning I was transplanted to 91a, Harley Street, W1. In a vast basement which once contained the wine treasures of medical or surgical specialists unknown to me was a Signal Office equipped with medium-power radio transmitters and receivers, teleprinters and batteries of hush-hush telephones, linked to GHQ which had its habitat in Knickerbocker Alley – another basement in the bowels of Selfridges of Oxford Street. A far cry from frosty Thirsk. Most of the men were Londoners. Married ones were allowed to sleep at home when off duty. The food was excellent. Our leisure activities were more varied and gratifying than those we had enjoyed in Paris at the beginning of the phoney war. We practically took over the Dover Castle in Weymouth Mews as our local pub, where nightly and sometimes mid-morningly we drank, sang and played darts with personalities of the nearby BBC. I well recall playing darts with Jean Metcalfe, now the wife of Cliff Michelmore. We had fun with Harry and his wife Auntie Maude. Harry had been a coachman in the Mews. Auntie Maude scrubbed stone stairs for the BBC. Daily she complained about her swarm of 'lary' daughters and her sore knees. On Auntie's birthday I gave her some thatcher's knee-pads. She put them on in the public bar of the Dover Castle, gave us a corker of a 'Knees up Mother Brown' and wept like a land-drain with joy. Bebe Daniels, wife of Ben Lyon, the original Hell's Angel, did humanitarian stints behind a counter of the Balfour Club in Great Portland Street. She smiled as she served food and drink to Jew and Gentile alike, and gave free tickets to the Allied Forces. We sat in the orchestra stalls of the best shows in London – at a time when German scientists in the Baltic research establishment at Peenemunde were devoting their wits to making bigger and better doodle-bugs to drop on London. We had already sampled block busters and had dug out lots of its victims, and were awaiting delivery of Vergeltungswaffe Zwei, the V2. It was good fun.

When our establishment grew we took over a large mansion just round the corner in Queen Anne Street, whose owner had evacuated and had left behind a black greyhound, plus a cook to act as house caretaker and canine comrade. Boozy and belligerent, he knew little of dogs. Thrice daily he over-fed Mick on thick steaks, with the result that instead of running and walking Mick waddled. Now and again I took Mick to Regent's Park where, in cavalry style, I lunged him on a long rein until his fat went and his speed returned. Mick was loth to leave me. On my week's leave to Wales I took him to Paddington Station, where a guard refused to let him ride with me in a coach.

'Put him in the guard's van. Tie him to that tin trunk!'

There was much noise when I walked the platform to find a seat. Mick followed, dragging the trunk. I decided to keep him company to Swansea, and stayed in the guard's van, thus losing valuable drinking time in the buffet bar. Mother-in-law Mary Jones was much put out when she saw my Mick.

'Cedric, bach! It's a milgy!'

Greyhound, whippets and those that ran them were not wanted at Tyrcoed.

'Put it in the greenhouse, out of sight!'

I hid Mick there in the presence of my son John and his cousins Peter and Michael. When they took him some food he bit the lot of them. I had told the boys that Mick was a direct descendant of champion Mick the Miller. The news leaked. In the evening a doggy-looking man came to talk in reverential whispers.

'Don't show, now. Give him a run against our dogs in the morning.'

Mick showed the other dogs how to run. The little man was so impressed that he offered me £9 for dog, collar and lead. After I had inspected the kennels to ensure Mick would have a good home – he was running to seed in London and I would not be able to care for him – I accepted the £9. Mick was quickly entered for two races at nearby Fforestfach, and won both. But next day the little man turned up with an anxious face, one dog collar and one lead.

''Aven't seen the ole dog, 'ave you, boyo?'

I had not. Mick has not been seen in South Wales to this day.

'Do you know the residence of the Prime Minister, Chequers?'

I was asked this question by a major of Guards, Armoured Division, on my return from Wales.

'Yes, it's in Buckinghamshire.'

'That's right! You will be going there each weekend that Mr Churchill is in residence. They will not be social visits.

You will go with a detachment of the Guards' Armoured Division to maintain communication between Chequers and War Office. It is called Exercise Elephant. Keep it under your hat. Here are the details.'

Gigantic guardsmen and armoured cars were responsible for the Prime Minister's personal safety, and we signallers for the communication. We attended Chequers at weekends where we slept on stable floors. Being an old cavalryman I felt much at home as well as highly honoured. Some of the Guards were not impressed and complained that in the big house were many servant's rooms, all unoccupied, and they thought they should be in them.

Mr Churchill spoke to me one morning. He caught me puggling an aerial rod down a mole run near one of his border plots.

'Are you fond of gardening?'

I said that I was more familiar with gardening than fond of it, because as a lad I had done much of it for little reward. He asked questions about my soldiering, and we swopped stories about places in Egypt and India, and about my old regiment the Royal Dragoons and his own, the 4th Royal Hussars. His eyes twinkled when I referred to the 4th as 'The Charsies'.

'What do you do in the evenings?'

'We play cards when off duty, on our beds in the stables.'

'Would you like to go to the pictures?'

I told him we were not allowed to leave Chequers while he was present. Next day we were invited to his drawing room. In the back row of chairs we sat behind Cabinet Ministers and top brass of the Services. News films were being shown about the Russian counter-offensive of 1942, when much ground had been regained. It was inspiring to see Mr Churchill clapping. After he set the pace the others joined in. I learned quite a bit at Chequers.

In 1943 London appeared to have been invaded – by the Americans. They swarmed in Soho, hosted in Holborn and rallied at Rainbow Corner like all the world and his wife. It was good to see them. They introduced us to Rye, bourbon and cigars; but kept all the women.

Mass migration, feverish activity and partial imprisonments were rife in the early weeks of spring 1944, to get into launching positions the hordes of Allied troops who were to invade the continent. Extraordinary steps had been taken to ensure that soldiers would not escape to London for a final fling. It was rumoured that all Scotsmen had been posted to the Southern Counties; all Englishmen to the Orkneys and the Welsh to the East Coast. That all married men had been posted to places remote from their wives. Whether this was the general pattern I will never know, but it seemed to be so in that Regimental Holding Unit at Thursley Camp, Godalming, Surrey, where I found myself folded like a wayward sheep within barbed wire entanglements surrounding the pines and larches of a fair-sized wood. Roll was called several times a day. Fatigues helped to pass the time as we camouflaged everything in sight. Diatribes from manuals of military law, with an accent on the penalties for desertion, were read to the new contingents that poured in daily. Troops and tanks abounded in woods and hedges, all set for D-Day. But there were loopholes, even in the barbed wire. I had been wire-cooped for over a month when I had an urge to escape to see some friends in London, and left word with a fellow sergeant that if a posting hatched out I could be contacted on a Primrose telephone number.

At 11.30 p.m. the telephone rang.

'Get back at the gallop. The balloon goes up tomorrow!'

I learned at Baker Street that because of an air raid the tube was closed – except to shelterers – and until the 'all clear' sounded not another train would run under the Thames. Hoping to avoid the death penalty for desertion I telephoned the guard room of St John's Wood Barracks and asked if drivers and vehicles were present, and was told to go and find out. I hitch-hiked to St John's Wood. To my delight my friend Driver Gilbert was present. I confessed that if he could not get me to Thursley before 0400 hours I would become a candidate for a Field General Court Martial for desertion. In five minutes Gilbert rounded up a 15 cwt truck.

'I'll get bloody shot for this. Don't know how much is in the tank, but I'll take you as far as I can. Must have enough to get me back.'

We crossed the Thames by Westminster Bridge and in the blackout drove till we found the Portsmouth Road. Neither of us had matches. After shinning up a war memorial which he had mistaken for a signpost – and there were no signposts then – Gilbert was told by a drunk that we were at Milford Cross. A flick of my fuel-less lighter gave enough light for Gilbert to look at the dash-board, to find he had not enough petrol to take him back to St John's Wood.

'That's torn it. We're both in it now, mate. See you in the glasshouse!'

We shook hands and wished each other luck. After I had plodded a mile or more along the Guildford by-pass I heard behind me the whine of a fast-driven jeep. The problem was how to stop it in a night as black as sin. I took a letter from my pocket and put it in my cheese-cutter hat, then flicked my lighter – hoping that the spark would be reflected for the driver to see a bit of a signal. I was in luck. The driver pulled up. He was the duty courier of the American Service which ran nightly from Oxford Street to Southampton.

'O.K., bud . . . hop in!'

He dropped me at Thursley Wood at 0245 hours.

'Watch out for the Heinies, bud, and fetch me back one of those French chicks.'

I groped to my tent in the pine wood, picked up my rifle, put on my pack and joined a shadowy cursing parade. The roll was just about to be called. I was in time to answer my name. We mounted the trucks, bound for Southampton.

It was a fine morning on 30 June. Four years had passed since we left France defeated and humiliated. On my way to Southampton I counted my blessings. I had not experienced the excitement of further active service overseas like my old colleagues who had gone on to Africa and Italy, but I counted myself fortunate in learning more about Britain than I would otherwise have learnt. Much of the time had been devoted to boring, repetitious basic training under commanders who had little understanding of the minds of professional soldiers. But I was thankful still to be in one piece. It was good to be alive and fit as our boat steamed across the English Channel with an escort of bustling smoking destroyers and some fighter aircraft of Coastal Command. So good in fact that despite the discomfort of a Mae West life jacket I soon went to sleep on the deck and did not waken until we were about to pull in to the mooring buoys of the uncompleted Mulberry harbour at Arromanches.

In a way I was sorry not to have been there earlier, on D-day, Tuesday 6 June. By this time the British Second Army had captured Bayeux. Caen was practically surrounded and our advance units had crossed the railway line and the River Odon on a narrowish front between Noyers and Caen. But we were bound for Bayeux, on foot. We marched along the beginnings of that great road where weapons, ammunition and other supplies were being hurtled at great speed to raise clouds of yellow dust. Much dust fell on us, but I was pleased to see it in thick coats upon the uniforms of sullen-looking German prisoners caged in wire to the right of the road. We marched up the rise from Arromanches and had our first glimpse of the twin spires of Bayeux Cathedral, the place where Queen Mathilde's tapestry had hung for so long to tell of a former invasion. Guns were thundering in the distance. We were marching towards them, and the Germans, in some trepidation.

For days we idly skulked in fields south of Bayeux awaiting orders to proceed towards Caen to become attached to the Guards Armoured or the 51st Division. Nightly we trembled in slit trenches alongside a battery of light ack-ack. Several times a night the Luftwaffe dropped visiting cards. Machine-gun bullets and steel splinters ricocheted from gun barrels before the ack-ack opened up to add to the din. I remember how we had complained when ordered to dig slit trenches; but we were soon glad of them, and repented the disobliging remarks we made to half a dozen overworked cooks who from vast Aldershot ovens produced the world's worst food. After the Luftwaffe's visits new earth had to be dug to build new ovens. Tired and hand-blistered from his daily digging, one cook was too weary to dig himself a protective trench and slept above the earth, for the last time. He was neatly sliced in two.

Caen was captured on 9 July, my brother Leslie's birthday. For four years he had been behind barbed wire in Germany as a POW. I thought of him and my two other brothers, as heavy bombers of RAF Bomber Command roared over us half-a-thousand strong in the early hours of 8 July to attack German positions north of Caen. I felt so pleased. Baby brother Frank (we called him Chaffy) had been cooped up six months in the siege of Tobruk and had left there for Burma to join Orde Wingate's 'Chindits'. Jack was still in Addenbrooke's Hospital, Cambridge. His tank and his knee had been shot to bits at St Valéry before he was stretcher-borne from Dunkirk.

Five major bombing attacks by heavy and fighter bombers of the 8th and 9th USAAF followed towards the end of July. Some were over a thousand strong. Unfortunately a British raid designed to help the U.S. First Army to cross the Periers-Saint-Lô road dropped its bombs too short and caused much resentment and heavy casualties in the British and Canadian Forces. Caen became a shambles of death and desolation. It had been such a pleasant friendly city, which I had visited four years earlier on my bicycle when I used to tour Manche from Cherbourg. I thought of that delightful May morning when I dismounted to take lunch at a table outside a Caen pavement café. Two charming young ladies served me a magnificent omelette, a garden-fresh salad and a bottle of wine. The proprietor was an old soldier of the 1914–18 war and wore the ribbon of the Croix de Guerre. He chatted with me, gave me a packet of Gaulois cigarettes and refused to take money for that meal. I thought if I had half a chance I would try to find out how he had fared in this man-made hell on earth. But on my own birthday, 5 August, we moved off in clouds of dust towards Falaise.

For a few days we oscillated between two small farms, one to the east of the Forét de Cinglais on the west bank of the River Laize about eighteen miles from Falaise, without doing anything useful. Each night heavy lorries moved off to the north to pick up supplies from Cherbourg. I decided to do a bit of hitch-hiking and boarded a truck one moonless night on a personal voyage of discovery. The driver assured me he would bring me back on the return trip. The journey was dusty and extremely uncomfortable, but just as dawn was breaking we were on the heights of Montagne du Roule whose five forts overlooked the port of Cherbourg. We went down the hill and into a totally different town from the one I had known in 1939–40. All the port facilities had been destroyed and the waterways were blocked with sunken ships. The fine tower and its clocks had been toppled by the Germans and the port rendered useless before Cherbourg was recaptured on 26 June.

I strolled round some of my old haunts near the Gare Maritime. The Hôtel du Casino was in bad shape; 11 rue Noyon was heavily battle-scarred, its windows sand-bagged and its door reinforced by a lolling, coloured infantryman of the U.S. Forces, with the widest grin and the whiskiest-laden breath of my experience. I asked him who the hell had given him leave to stand in my doorway, and said the rue Noyon had been my home for some of the opening months of the war. He grinned even wider, and grabbed my hand.

'Welcome home, bud. Come right in. WE ain't got no chicks, but there's lotser booze.'

A dozen or so of his coloured chums had taken over our old home. Some were playing cards. Others reclined on those self-same beds we had fashioned from wood and wire-netting to form bunks. Whisky was poured in unbelievably liberal measures; stories were exchanged and I was given a whole box of cigars before they took me to their favourite *estaminet* – which used to be mine – in the rue au Blé. It was delightful and yet distressing to sit with them, to see their happy black faces; for behind them I could see the grinning dials of Doug Selway, Cecil Sugare, Monty Williams and Alf Warne, and others of the old gang of 48 Teleprinter Operating Section. The former proprietor of the nearby Hôtel de Tournville had been killed when the Germans wrecked the Gare Maritime. His grandson Pierre, a vivacious young lad of eleven years who used to call me 'Mon oncle Spiko', had died with him. I was very upset to hear this news from Alice Lavalois, who still survived to change bed linen – for the Americans. Those American lads could not have been kinder. When they offered to drive me back to my unit I accepted. We made two stops for food and drink, for which they paid, at Valognes and Carentan. There was not much left of those formerly pleasant places. In a way I was glad to be back in the comparative peace of the forest, to do a bit of thinking. To my surprise my absence had remained undetected.

Two days before the main attack of the Allies began on 14 August we established a new radio link and communication with a new H.Q. We left the cover of the forest and operated on the move during a slow advance through small woods along the east bank of the River Laize. Except for food breaks I sat at my set continuously for over forty-eight hours; wireless operators were still a bit thin on the ground. Even through my heavily padded headphones I could hear that awful din of the assault on Falaise. Heavy bombers roared overhead. There were nerve-shattering bomb blasts and the thunder of gunfire. Crystal Palace had never known such a display of fireworks. Lightning-like flashes stained the night clouds with incessant bursts of coloured light ranging from saffron yellow to deep carmine. From the bombs came Mars-orange sulphur flashes and electric-blue flaring from cobalt. The earth heaved and quaked as it danced a fiery protest.

I finished my long stint and stepped from the gin palace. I was not in the least fatigued or frightened. Instead, like most of us, I had a feeling of intense excitement and elation, perhaps because we appreciated that those barbarians were now receiving a first-class dose of their own rough medicine.

Leaning against a nearby tree was a motor cycle. I had not been across the saddle of one since I learned to ride at Bulford Camp. It coughed to life with the first kick. I aimed it in the general direction of higher ground beyond the fringe of the wood, where I hoped to get a grandstand seat for the fireworks. But I never reached that point. Had I not been so inquisitive I would not now be drawing a War Disability Pension for defective vision. I shall never know what hit me, but I remember regaining consciousness – under the impression that I had got my deserts and was in Heaven. But it was not the voice of angels after all. Merely a bunch of Taffy soldiers singing 'Calon Lân'.

Bed-bound, bandaged and blinded, I was in the field hospital below Bayeux.

'You'll be all right,' said the sister. 'A bit of a crack on the head. Your eyes are a bit wonky. It's mostly shock. Don't worry!'

Twelve days passed by before she took off the bandages. I was relieved to discover that I could see twice as much as before. I had double vision. People and objects danced around before merging into indefinable hazes. Pains came to the back of my eyes when I concentrated on focusing – trying to fit the dancing jig-saws into some visual pattern. The eye specialist came with good news.

'We are sending you back to England. Moorfields Eye Hospital will soon put you right.'

On 4 September 1944 I was bound for Southampton – the only passenger on a TLC. Like a Monte Carlo croupier I wore over my brow a green eye-shield. Strapped to the upper-piling swivel of my rifle was a souvenir for my son John. It was a part-worn steel helmet which bore in Gothic symbols the name and unit of the former wearer, 'Ernst Bogue, 1 SS Panzer Corps'. Shrapnel had made two holes in it, at entrance and exit, around which were splinterings of bone, dried blood and bits of yellow hair. I was sure John would love to show it to his schoolboy friends before I planted a geranium in it, which I did, a Paul Crampell Scarlet.

Apart from my AB64 I had no papers. The RTO at Southampton had fewer. He would not believe me. Instead of hurtling me to Moorfields Hospital, he made out my rail warrant to the Signal Training Centre, Catterick Camp, Yorkshire, the depot of the Royal Signals. For a long time the Catterick pen-pushers searched for instructions, but in vain. After making myself a nuisance, I was examined by an eye specialist, who swiftly demeaned my medical category A1 to C2 and insisted that I should be posted to London forthwith.

Virtually unemployable I used to mount and march each morning from my old haunt St John's Wood Barracks, NW8 to Moorfields Eye Hospital near Old Street Underground where in the expert hands of charming Miss Pugh I received a protracted course of orthoptic treatment. For hours at a stretch I sat on a stool and peered into the lenses of an optical instrument not unlike the Barr & Stroud Rangefinder used by artillerymen. Two pictures had to be dropped into slots to begin the performance. Into the right flank slot a picture of a multi-coloured parrot. Into the left flank slot the picture of an empty birdcage. By twiddling knobs and concentrating visually on both targets I had to put pretty Polly into her cage.

During this time the German fighting forces surrendered unconditionally (7 May 1945), but I have forgotten my impressions of VE Day – probably because I was still receiving treatment in hospital – though I may have drunk the double whiskies which my 15-deg. convergence deficiency caused me to see when I ordered only singles.

Bored beyond endurance with inactivity, I applied to my C.O. for permission to undertake light employment of a non-military nature outside the barracks; adding that it might assist me in finding employment in civvy street if my eyes did not respond to treatment. Within two days – partly because I had sounded out the prospects with a prospective employer – most of my non-hospital hours were spent in Bakewell's electrical shop in St John's Wood High Street. There, with aged craftsman Mr (Tod) Slaughter, I repaired wireless sets and created minor masterpieces of candelabra from a furtively-collected assortment of crystal pendants that doodle-bugs had blasted from major candelabra in those socially esteemed flats near Regent's Park. I repaired many sets, created many lampshades, made hosts of friends and much money.

The rot set in when Bakewell's friend Bernard came on to the peaceful but industrious scene. This excessively patriotic Englishman spoke impeccable French and German, drove fast motor-cars, and his capacity for drinking whisky was boundless. His main object in life appeared to be to search for excuses to celebrate. Providence galloped across his front when he gleaned the news that an atomic bomb dropped by an American plane had burst its Uranium-235 explosive at 1,500 feet over Hiroshima to raze four square miles of the city. I have never seen anyone look so pleased. We celebrated. We repeated the performance on 9 August when the next atomic bomb destroyed Nagasaki; but the best celebration was after the announcement that on 14 August General Itagaki had surrendered to Admiral Mountbatten in Singapore.

Well lit up with whisky, adorned with red, white and blue rosettes, we drove to a pub standing well back from the road in Walmer Green. Instead of entering by the door, Bernard crashed through the French windows and made a public announcement. 'Ladies and gentlemen of Walmer Green, I salute you. My ingenious friend here,' he pointed to me, 'has just beaten the Japanese. It was he who designed the bomb. Meet Professor Spike Mays. Drinks all round!'

We were lucky to emerge alive. And when we did – much later – Bernard tried to drive back to his home in Swiss Cottage. We were on the grass verges of the Finchley Road more than off them before he got his bearings and could keep on the glide-path. Turning a corner at Swiss Cottage we had to avoid a large American truck bearing the Stars and Stripes and a gang of celebrating G.Is. Bernard swung the wheel, we mounted a pavement and I saw the tree aiming itself at the car bonnet. The next thing I knew was a smell of ether, and pain. Bernard was severely winded and bruised by the steering column.

About forty stitches were made in my head and hands. Bernard was massaged considerably. But the moment we were put on a milk diet we discharged ourselves from Hampstead Hospital. 'At your own risk!' said the Matron, as she gave me permission to telephone Natalie Stuart (Mrs Bakewell's daughter) to fetch me my uniform. The suit I had been wearing was drenched in blood.

We had two more celebrations. One for the complete write-off of Bernard's motor-car, and a longer one on 2 September for the signing of peace. Somehow we got separated, and I have not seen or heard of him since.

It occurred to me that Vera might like to be present when I was issued with my de-mob suit. She waited a long time outside the Albany Barracks as the tailor tried to find something to fit me, which he never did. But I put it on to leave the barracks and Vera and I had our picture taken in a St John's Wood photographer's. This was in the early days of October 1945, but until my formal discharge (after my leave) I could wear my four Long Service and Good Conduct chevrons (for nineteen years of undetected crime), the Indian G.S. Medal, the Defence Medal, the 1939–45 Medal, the 1939 Star, the France and Germany Star and the Long Service and Efficiency Medal of the Territorial Army.

It was not much to write home about, but then, I had no home. Something had to be done about it!

FIFTEEN

Civvy Street

QMS BAILLIE handed me my last ever furlough form.

'You've got leave for three months, ration an' clothin' allowance, plus yer bleedin' blood money, mate.'

He counted it out slowly on the army-blanketed table, ninety pounds, more than enough to go to Wales with Vera to collect my son John, to take us to the fields and woods of Ashdon and get the war, its hurts and separations out of our systems. But I received a heart-rending, kindly reminder from my father-in-law Joe Jones a few days before we left Loughor. He called me into his workshop and gave me a cardboard box filled with three-inch squares of glossy papers. Between them were powderings of gold-leaf.

'I thought you would want to paint it, Cedric, bach. Here's the brush, some linseed oil and turps. I'll show how to mix it.'

During my absence he had engaged the stone mason to cut in the family tombstone at Moriah Chapel's burial plot the name of our dead son Glyn. Not just 'Mays', but the surname Glyn made for himself, 'Jones-Mays' because he loved his grandfather. Four of Joe's children already had their names on that stone, under the words 'Suffer little children to come unto me'. Joe had painted them. It was my turn now. It needed not a galaxy of artistic talents to brush gold-leaf into those deep, newly chiselled letters and figures. Merely a steady hand and a pair of dry eyes. I had neither. But I managed.

GLYN JONES-MAYS
Born 11 July 1938
Died 3 May 1941

It was a labour of love.

We could see wisps of smoke coming from the chimney. There was a hungry-making smell of newly-baked scones as we dismounted from Len Martin's motor and tried to surprise Mother by tip-toeing round the little path of Brick and Stone Villa at Reuben's Corner. A forlorn hope . . . Mother could detect a stray cat by its footsteps at a hundred paces. And there she was at the back door, all oven-flushed and eye-damped with joy. Father was on his allotment as usual, but soon came in to welcome us with complaints and excuses. 'Pity you're so late. The peas and beans are done, barrin' a few long pithy-uns!'

It was so nice to be home again. I looked out of the window and saw the old mill. The welcome from the elements was far better than I had expected. Although there was a bit of a nip in the clear air, there was the usual lucidity of light. Blue skies were on parade with ceremonial puffs of white cloud; the sun shone on the new thatch of Wuddy Smith's old cottage, now owned by an American, and on the familiar tiles of the Bonnett Inn, less than three hundred yards away.

We drew up chairs to the table with the lion's claw base, for a 'real, owd appetiser'. News gushed from Mother as she missed the cup with her excited tea-pouring . . .

'Jack's knee is on the mend . . . Frank is back in England . . . Fon (my brother Leslie) has started work as a driver . . . Poppy's got a cottage at Church End . . . Lots of the boys are home, but you wouldn't know half of them now, Ced. You've been away too long.'

After the meal my father managed to get a word in. Characteristically, he said the Bonnett was open, and Threadgold would be pleased to see me. We moved off, lapping our tongues in pleasant anticipation of pints of Greene, King's best ale. It was so nice to be home.

Vera had worked at Paris House, the Gorseinon draper's shop, for some of the six years of separation. She saved her earnings, bits of the army allowance, and my balance surplus of civil service pay. Most of my £90 was still intact, but without a home and with our furniture in store, we had to get down to basics. We sorted it out in our first week, in those lovely woodlands, Home and Langley, so conducive to thought and day-dreaming. The Post Office at Hayes did not expect me to resume work until the end of my leave. I telephoned Bakewell's shop in St John's Wood, asking if they could use me for a few weeks, and was delighted when they said I could continue wireless repairs, although I was over fifty miles away. We had no motor-car. There were but few in Ashdon village and the little Ashdon Halt Station was two miles from our cottage. I used to walk those two miles to catch the London train, clad in overalls, much to the amusement of the villagers, and carrying my kit of instrument mechanic's tools in a box I made, with dove-tailed joints, leather thongs to hold the tools, nickel clasps, a lock and two keys. Although not yet formally discharged from the army, I felt a bit like a civvy and had my civvy clothes on under my overalls.

I did not always behave like a civvy. Much work awaited me at Bakewell's. One of my first jobs called forth letters of denunciation. A kindly Jewish gentleman asked if I would go with him right away to repair his silent radiogram. He whisked me off to a huge flat opposite St John's Wood tube station where ankle deep in soft carpets I listened to his tale of woe.

'I am a singer. I have to go off for singing lessons now. Make yourself at home. Help yourself to whisky, and you'll find cigars in that box.'

The radiogram was repaired before he reached the lift. A lead had broken off the switch. I did not take the whisky, but fancied a cigar. It was so luxurious sitting in that deep armchair puffing out a cloud of millionaire-scented smoke. Someone had told me it was not the done thing to knock the ash from a good cigar, and that the length of rigid ash was a positive indication of cost and quality. Mine had a good one-and-a-half inches of quality before signs of drooping set in. Not wishing to desecrate the costly carpet I searched for a common ash tray. On a window ledge all a-bristle with gleaming silverware stood an ornate bronze bowl; the only receptacle in sight not holding rich roses and costly carnations. Into that bowl I flicked my ash, then beetled back to Bakewell's to make out a bill for ten bob. The letter came next morning, to say the radiogram was working as good as new, but the owner would like to get his hands on the infidel who had added ash to the ashes of his departed ancestors. It turned out all right in the end . . . well, almost all right. Having received my carefully written apology, the gentleman sent for me. He sat me in the best armchair, plied me with whisky, gave me another cigar and an ash tray. 'You may keep the ash tray as a souvenir.' But he got his revenge. I pretended to enjoy his raucous rendering of Tosti's 'Parted'.

Mrs Bakewell who owned the shop was a Yorkshire widow. She had bought a fine piano for the musical education of her two daughters who were now grown up and no longer interested in crochets and quavers. Until I put my fingers on the smooth ivory keys of that mellifluous masterpiece by R. Gors Kallmann of Berlin its voice had been silent for years. Not that I could play it. I could pick out a lullaby with my right hand, but neighbours complained that lullabies were not intended to act as reveilles. Weeks passed before I could vamp with my left hand, and I came to the conclusion that four brains were essential for piano playing, one for each hand, and one for each foot. But I was very fond of that seven-octave, upright grand.

'When you get rich, you can buy it,' said Mrs Bakewell. 'I've just had it valued. It's worth £200.' I said I would think about it.

We had not saved enough money to put down a deposit on a house by the time I resumed work at the Post Office. Instead we found digs, a couple of rooms, with Mr Knight who lived almost opposite our pre-war abode. There was no room to turn a screwdriver, but we stuck it for three months. Two days before starting work I decided to spy out the land on a social visit, and was sufficiently misguided as to enter the overseer's room. Bill Rayment, promoted to that lofty estate during my active service elsewhere, had gone to the bank to get cash for the tills. Before going to chat to a couple of postmen I hung my new de-mob trilby on a peg. In five minutes Bill returned, looking extremely important with the black Gladstone bag chained to his near-fore.

'Good morning, Bill,' said I, proffering a friendly hand which was ignored. I saw his beady eyes light on my hat. 'Is that yours?'

'Yes,' said I. 'It's a farewell present from the army. Do you like it?'

'Take it orf at once. That's the overseer's peg!'

This is not the best of welcomes, I thought, and then I remembered how well he liked his mid-morning pint, and invited him to pop over to the Old Crown at my expense. Bill beamed all the way to the pub and began a diatribe about his two promotions during six years of war. Not only had he become an overseer, but he had gained two pips as a lieutenant in the Home Guard and seemed sorry that the war had ended to stop him gaining his captaincy.

Len the landlord bade me good morning and welcome. I called up two pints and reminded Bill that officers and gentlemen always doffed their hats in the saloon bar. Bill snorted, but removed his hat. I christened his two promotions by pouring two pints over his head. Not the best way to start off again in civvy street, but I thought a damper would not come amiss after that pomp and circumstance.

But during the war Bill Rayment had met his Waterloo, Arthur Briden told me later. Bill ruled his Home Guard squad of pike-and-pepper warriors with the discipline exerted on recruits in his colour service days, when he had been a footdrill instructor in the Diehards (Middlesex Regiment), and the lads hated his guts. One day Bill's army was called upon to safeguard the Hayes Post Office. War had been declared on Hayes Home Guard (the Red army) by the Home Guard of Southall (the Blue army). Bill marshalled his forces, issued them with pikes and pepperpots, borrowed reinforcements from Heston and Isleworth, and put the lot on guard around all roads leading to Hayes Post Office. There were so many Home Guardsmen encircling the area that it seemed impossible to slip in a cigarette paper between them. But the Blue army of Southall was unsporting, to say the least. Lieutenant Bill Rayment himself waved on the coke lorry to Nield Road, and actually stopped other traffic entering Nield and St Anselm's roads as he guided the canvas-hooded coke-carrier over the Hayes Post Office coal-hole. But it was not coke which poured down the hole, it was the Blue army of Southall, and in five seconds flat Hayes Post Office was captured, from the inside.

It was not until 12 April 1946 that we could afford to sign all those solicitor's forms for our house in Nield Road, about four hundred yards from Hayes Post Office, which we bought from a postman who had to transfer to Folkestone. Arthur Briden, on leave from the RAF pending his demobilisation, helped me move in our furniture from store. It was a blessing that Vera had gone to Wales for that weekend, because the old Post Office table again reared its head. I wanted to put it in the box-room. We tried to get it there via the small kitchen, but the wind blew the back door shut behind us and we were imprisoned for half an hour's good cursing until neighbours released us.

'How about takin' it fru the upstairs window wiv a rope an' a ladder?' asked Arthur. 'It'll be upstairs when we gets it in the 'ouse.'

We borrowed a ladder and a rope. I tied the rope to a table leg and pulled from the bedroom window as Arthur tried to push the table up the ladder. I whisked him off the ladder twice. At the third attempt we managed to get the table to bay-window level, but the little mat on which I stood shot from under me on the slippery new linoleum. One window pane was broken. Arthur crashed down with the table on top of him and sprained his ankle. Neighbours closed doors and windows as ripe RAF curses rang out. We gave up, then went to the Old Crown for a pint. Landlord Len chipped in... 'The only way is to take it fru the french window, fru the 'all an' up the bleedin' apples an' pears, me ole mate.'

We got it into the hall. Much new paper was torn from walls and paint from banisters before the table wedged itself between wall and banisters. I had had more than enough. With my new tenon saw I carefully cut three inches off each of the legs, and the table went up the stairs without touching the sides. We plonked it down in the box-room, under the window where I could have light for my labourings. We wiped off our sweat.

'You'll go all humpty-backed working on a short-arsed table like that, mate,' said Arthur. I enjoined him to maintain silence and to watch my artistry as I drilled holes in the cut-offs, then screwed them back to their former positions with 4-inch screws. We could hardly see the joins. But Vera spotted them and was furious about the havoc and my table. She did not want it in the box-room. 'Take it up the garden and put it in the workshop,' she demanded. I gave the matter great thought, but two days afterwards I received a shock. Standing smack in the middle of my workshop was the table, screwed-on legs and all. I asked Vera who had moved it.

'I did,' said she, with that cunning look worn by women who win.

'Who helped you?'

'No one . . . but I did not do it in one trip.'

'How the hell can you move one table in more than one trip?'

'Easily,' said she, with an even more cunning look. 'And if you and that Air Force fool had used your eyes, you could have done it without all that damage.'

'What the devil have eyes got to do with it?'

'Everything . . . if you had used yours you would have found four butterfly nuts underneath. When they are unscrewed the top lifts off.'

Later that year I took great delight in chopping up the table and in puggling the last glowing embers as they lit John's fireworks on 5 November.

Apart from the Falaise motor cycle incident when I was blinded through wishing to see too much, and the perils of VJ-Day celebrations, my life has been caught up with accidents from which I have escaped physically unscathed. Others have borne the brunt.

Knowing how deeply I doted upon her Gors Kallmann piano, realising I could never raise £200 to buy it, and aware that the piano was the only silent thing in her flat, Mrs Bakewell pitied my poverty and asked her daughter Natalie to write to me to arrange a convenient collection date. I could purchase my heart's desire for a mere £60. Vera was overjoyed, and promised to buy it for me as a reunion present. It was with great enthusiasm and speed that I appointed a haulage contractor, who said, 'Next Tuesday, mate?' Mrs Bakewell agreed, and suggested to avoid stairs and steps in her basement flat that it would be advisable to remove the basement window from its frame. The removals man rushed to St John's Wood. Without a word to a living soul he whipped out the window, and whipped the piano into his pantechnicon and then to my home. Later in the week I received a telephone call from Natalie, who tore me to shreds for my discourtesy. Unfortunately –

and in the depths of winter when her mother was bed-bound with bronchitis – my man had rushed off without replacing the window. Frost reigned over St John's Wood for weeks, partly because Mrs Bakewell's bronchitis blossomed into pneumonia. Finding the lost chord would have been child's play compared with my attempts to write a suitable apology. But Mrs Bakewell had a magnificent sense of humour. She said she saw the funny side. Not so my new neighbours, who were quite disenchanted when I did my scales and five-finger exercises late at night, the only time when Post Office hours permitted me to touch the keyboard.

Screwed to the wall behind the Post Office counter was a cupboard with 120 shelves. Upon each shelf, in alphabetical and numerical order, reposed up to a dozen forms of various hues, shapes and dimensions. Not all were intended for the general public. Couched in gobbledegook, a language which seemed to have been invented to make the obvious appear difficult, some had an instructional content for laymen. I liked the one intended to be helpful about radio interference, one which caused a lady of seventy-four years (my mother) to puggle into the orifices of a live mains socket with a 14-inch steel knitting needle. Fortunately, she had been wearing her gardening boots at the time, a pair of rubber Wellingtons, and had been insulated from mother earth. The instruction read thus:

> LOOKING FOR THE CAUSE OF INTERFERENCE IN YOUR OWN HOME
>
> HOUSE WIRING. If the interference seems to be connected with someone walking about in some part of the house it is probably due to a fault in the electrical wiring. Make sure that plugs and sockets are clean and check whether the interference is affected by putting switches on and off.

Mother narrowly escaped electrocution. Being an East Anglian she persevered, but was not much comforted by the next paragraph of the P.O. form, which gave advice about the whistling noises in her old wireless set.

> If a whistle occurs, particularly after dark, it is probably due to a foreign station. Apart from slight adjustments to the tuning or positioning of your receiver, and giving attention to your aerial, there is nothing that can be done locally to overcome this type of interference, but the Post Office tries to get the interference stopped by complaining to the country concerned.

She wrote at the gallop to our hamlet postmistress, and asked her to complain to Australia. Sick to the teeth with cricket (a Test match was on for most of the week) she had failed to tune in to 'The Archers'.

I continued to take an increasing interest in the local and distant affairs of the Union of Post Office Workers, and several consecutive years was elected Indoor Secretary, Welfare Officer, and Annual Conference Delegate. In the latter capacity I was delighted to meet old friends in the main conference halls of Great Britain, where we mounted rostrums and did verbal battle on behalf of our colleagues. Another honorary post came my way when I was elected Financial Secretary for Outer London Districts. But in my own job I graduated at a good snail's gallop from writing duties and performed occasional stints as Assistant Overseer and Counter Superintendent.

Our house became paper-packed and book-bulgy. Through reading and writing on Economics, British European History and Human Relations in Industry, I suffered spasmodic attacks of reader's retina and writer's writhe. Always at the back of my mind were the words of Bill Williams, 'Remember this . . . "Bread is food for the body, flowers are food for the soul, and books are food for the mind".' I felt I needed all nourishment within reach to catch up. Poverty had prevented my attendance at grammar school. War had prevented my going up to Oxford by scholarship. Lack of formal education had denied me commissioned rank in the army. Determined not to be beaten, I put my hand and mind to personal improvement, neglected my family and was practically out of communication with Vera and John for two years.

John brought me to my senses when Vera was admitted to Hillingdon Hospital. He was left to the mercilessness of my culinary capers which in the main consisted of ex-military fry-ups and bully beef. A sad blow after Vera's excellent cooking. John declared that never again did he wish to clap eyes on bacon and bully (we usually had it three times a day). He insisted that vegetables should be served but once, immediately after being boiled, and not always bubble-and-squeaked. He clamoured for puddings and soup. Now, I could cope with soup, and I made some; hoping it would seethe sufficiently to be body-building and palatable on John's return from school for his midday meal. Concocted from King Edward potato stock, bits of crisp bacon rind and a can of processed peas, it looked a bit frail and tasted like the English Channel. A sprig of mint altered the flavour. Pearl barley did little to thicken the liquid. There was a reason. In the tin marked 'pearl barley' was a white powder. Under the impression that the rice-like grains had been ground to flour by the back-room wizards of the Co-op, I shot into the mixture two tablespoon loads. It seemed not to thicken. But oh how it fizzed!

John tasted, spat and spoke.

'It's awful, Dad . . . I won't eat it!'

'Oh yes, you will. Every drop. I have slaved over a hot stove and am late for work. Down the hatch, or not another bite until your mother comes out of hospital next week!'

John ate the lot. He was home an hour before his usual time. I accused him of playing hookey.

'Honest, Dad . . . I've been to school. They sent me home.'

'Why?'

'Making rude noises and stinks.'

John's indisposition was diagnosed when I told Vera about it that evening at visiting time. She nearly rolled out of her hospital bed. Her pearl barley tin contained bicarbonate of soda.

Incredibly, the postmaster looked even more worried than usual.

'Er, Mr Mays, just a minute. A man at the public counter has just seen you through the window. He'd like to have a word. Didn't give his name, but said something about knowing you when you were a spy. Hope it's all right!'

It was very much all right. Through the window I could see in all his ugliness Jigger Lee. We had known each other in Egypt, India and France, but I did not expect to see him again. Only the week before, Mrs Nicole Vyvyan had come into the Post Office to draw her widow's pension. Her husband Guy, one of our bright boys with fluent French, who had been commissioned and transferred to Intelligence, was shot after parachuting with the 6th Airborne Division on the Périers ridge. Nicole had heard that Jigger had been killed. I walked round the back of the office, crept up behind him and poked him one in the ribs. He spun round with fists at the high port, then much to the consternation of two female counter clerks he addressed me in the endearing terms of old soldiers.

'You wicked old bastard, Spike. What are you doing here?'

'None of that rough stuff, sir. You are not in the army now. I have been asked to escort you from the premises. Please come with me.'

His brows furrowed with ferocity, but unfurled with delight when I added, 'Hurry up, they're open!' Postmaster Hopkins had given me the day off. We were in the Old Crown less than five minutes to learn that we had been living in the same town for several years. Within a month – after I had taken him to a couple of meetings to prove that despite his exterior he was moderately harmless and that sponsors would put in a Christian word for him – Jig was sworn in a member of the local branch of the Fellowship of the Services, an ex-servicemen's association which catered for all ranks. Once a month we used to meet in a back room of the Royal Standard, Coldharbour Lane to gossip about old times. The Union Jack was spread on the table. On our national flag there reposed one Bible, two bayonets and four highly polished shell-cases holding candles, the only illumination for the short ritual of remembrance.

We were sixty strong, a mixture of officers and Other Ranks, the hale and hearty, the halt, lame and the blind. We had a brace of Royal Marines with three legs and three eyes between the twain; horse-smelly types from the Royals, Scots Greys and the Inniskilling Dragoons; sailors abounded, and there were heavily-moustached types from the Royal Air Force, from Wincos to Erks, and a majority from the PBI.

To enter that room after sampling the sullen silence of civilians was an inspiration. We had all shared the common danger and spoke a language of our own and used to look forward to the last Tuesday of each month. Sometimes we indulged in sing-songs in which all had to take part by individual contribution – at the beginning of the evening. We would all be singing at the end. It was the custom for recruits to give a story about an actual service experience. Line-shooting was out.

Jigger brought the house down with his maiden speech which began something like this.

'It was in the winter of 1924 at Catterick Camp. I was the only signalman there with a private motor cycle. Once in a while I would get weekend leave and go off to York, to meet friends and have some decent grub. One weekend I came across a motor cyclist who appeared to be in trouble. His bike was propped up on the grass verge. He was buffeting his arms because it was bitterly cold and, apart from the light of my headlamp, as black as a nigger's arse. I pulled up.

'"What's up, mate? Got a puncture?"

'"No . . . no lights."

'"I've got a tin of carbide in my saddle-bag. Hang on."

'"I've got carbide, but no water."

'Well, I looked round, but there wasn't a house for miles, so I gave the lad some good advice and told him to piss in the container.

'"Well, under the circumstances I cannot."

'"Well, I can spare you a drop. Hold the lamp."

'The lad held the lamp at the appropriate height. I damped his carbide, applied a match and there was light. He said he was going to York, so I suggested we rode together for company. When we got to a pub I asked him in for a pint, but he said he'd prefer a ginger wine. I ordered a pint and his perishing ginger wine, and told him to take his scarf, helmet and goggles off, otherwise he wouldn't get the benefit when he went out in the cold. To my surprise he whipped the lot off with one flick, and a yard-and-a-half of yellow hair fell down his back. The HE was a bloody SHE.'

There were claps all round, but Jig held up his hand for silence and continued.

'I apologised for being a bit blunt, but she said she didn't mind. She was a nurse and had four grown brothers and was broad-minded. We had more drink in York and swopped addresses. I used to write to her regularly. One day she reminded me she had a birthday coming up the straight. I asked some of the local Casanovas what sort of present I should buy her, and got bloody peculiar suggestions. But one day in the Catterick Store I found the very thing. I wrapped it up with a birthday card on which I wrote:

> '"Happy birthday, Elizabeth. May this small gift preserve you from the perils of darkness."'

Jig sat down and reached for his pint, but Lennard had not heard enough.

'Come on, you bloody scoundrel, tell us what was in that parcel.'

All eyes were on Jig as he stood up and gave me a wink.

'It's a pity ladies aren't allowed in this room. If they were I'd soon show you. In the saloon bar there is a lady in a red coat. Liz, my wife. If one of you would go and ask her, she'd probably tell. If she doesn't I'll buy drinks all round.'

Curly Spratley dashed into the saloon bar, then dashed back again, almost crippled with laughter.

'It's the truth, lads. Liz is Mrs Lee. Her birthday gift was a tin funnel.'

Our club was a kind of Freemasonry of the Services. We did things for each other; found jobs for the unemployed, dug gardens and clipped hedges and lawns for the wounded, and paid visits to those in hospital. One of our star turns was Harold Pooley, the sole survivor of German butchery when the Wehrmacht machine-gunned prisoners of war. Very badly wounded, Harold was long in hospital; but his health improved when he was selected to give evidence against German officers at the Nuremburg Trials. His book *The Vengeance of Private Pooley* was a great success and a film was made of it.

Apart from the monthly meeting up with old comrades, and playing cricket twice a week for the civil service, my only relaxations were Trade Union business and individual swotting. But in 1951 the gods were good to me the night we returned from my summer leave in Wales.

SIXTEEN

Newbattle Abbey College

NO LETTER-BOX could have been more stuffed with paper than ours when we returned that night. Letters a fortnight old had seeped to the hall, plus a copy of *The Post*. Vera went through the letters like lightning, and looked sad. I had seen the envelopes and knew they contained bills for rates, gas, electricity, water, and did not wish to know. We had no money. She brightened when she read that small paragraph in *The Post*, which invited essays on a 'National Wages Policy', whatever that meant. The winner could go to one of three places. To Ruskin, England, to Aberystwyth, Wales, or to Newbattle Abbey, Scotland.

'Look at this, Cedric. If you write and win you might get to college after all.'

'Let us eat first.'

Vera unwrapped the bakestones Mam had made for us, and the Welsh ham, and those round red-ripe tomatoes from Nhad's greenhouse, as I laid the cloth and John filled the kettle. Knives, forks and spoons; plates, cups and saucers, for us three, when there used to be four. I thought about the plight of ill-paid people like me as I laid them. Although I had never been out of work, and had always worked for the State, I was flat broke. It occurred to me, if anyone was justified in writing about wages, or the lack of them, it was myself. The meal was delicious. Vera and John yawned and went to bed. I got out my pen. It was the closing date for the essay competition, but I sent a note explaining that I had only just seen the advertisement, and enclosed my contribution all the same.

A fortnight afterwards a letter invited me to UPW House, Crescent Lane, Balham. I had been short-listed for the scholarship. I approached Crescent Lane with trepidation, to find on my arrival that my fears were groundless.

A panel of kindly, considerate gentlemen – including a benign professor from Harlech – swiftly put me at ease. Although there were many questions, skilfully framed, to discover whether I was intent on learning and had the intention of putting it into useful channels, the dreaded ordeal proved nothing more harmful than an exchange of views and a pleasant chat – aided and abetted by tea and sticky buns. I was questioned on my essay, in which I had said it was balderdash to introduce a National Wages Policy when it would never be possible to assess the relative value to the community, in terms of reward, between counter clerks and Counts, master builders and mannequins, postmasters and prostitutes; that to my certain knowledge gangs of charming but illiterate Irishmen, who were still digging up the pleasant smallholdings and horticultural plots of Heathrow to lay down concrete runways, had been denied by St Patrick the simple wit necessary to make out money order forms to send weekly sums of £30 to £40 to their dependants. Instead, they had to rely for the completion of the forms upon Post Office counter clerks whose wages seldom reached £10 per week. I had ended by stating that the ancient Indian adage about the pen being mightier than the sword was even more balderdashy. I had used pen, sword and the shovel. But in terms of wage-earning the English pen was puny compared with the Irish shovel. We discussed this at some length, then the Welsh professor asked my opinion of his race. He smiled when I said that I had married one of the tribe and had not regretted the circumstance.

They all smiled. We had more tea and sticky buns.

The letter came within a week. If the Post Office would grant me leave I could begin my formal education at Newbattle Abbey College, Dalkeith – at the age of forty-four years.

The GPO opened up its heart – if not its purse – by granting me leave (Class C – unpaid) for the duration of my absence, and guaranteed my seniority and entitlement to pension would remain unimpaired. But the UPW provided a grant of £300 to cover some of the costs of the academic year. In October 1951 I packed my bags for Edinburgh. Apart from the grant, my income ceased. My expenses were about to be doubled because we were still paying off the mortgage on our house. Thinking it unwise to uproot John from school again, and to keep the financial flag flying, albeit at lower than half-mast, Vera took a full-time job in a local factory, and wished me luck.

Newbattle Abbey, situated in the valley of the River Esk near Dalkeith, Midlothian, about eight miles from Edinburgh, was the gift of the late Marquess of Lothian. Residential Adult Colleges similar in character and purpose already existed, in a limited number, in England and Wales, but Newbattle Abbey was the first to be instituted north of the Border. On 18 May 1935, a largely attended gathering, representing all interested parties, was, by the invitation of Lord Lothian, held at the Abbey. Lord Elgin, Chairman of the Carnegie United Kingdom Trust, was authorised to offer £10,000 towards the cost of adapting the Abbey as a Residential College; and the then Secretary for Scotland, Sir Godfrey Collins, announced an annual government grant on a capitation basis of about £25 a year for each full session pupil. Sir Robert Rait for the York Trustees also promised five bursaries of £60 each.

During the next year the Executive Committee reported a sum of over £12,000 received or promised, of which £5,000 each was donated by Lord Lothian and Dr J. D. Pollock. The College opened in 1937, but was requisitioned in 1939 by the War Department for army education. In October 1950

Newbattle Abbey College resumed its civil activities – to provide for the needs of those like myself who, having been engaged for years in hum-drum but essential avocations, desired the opportunity of a wider and fuller education.

Briefly stated, men and women of at least eighteen years of age were eligible for admission. Its purpose was, and is, to develop the capacities of its members and to prepare them to meet more effectively the trials and tribulations of a modern democracy. I soon discovered that the method of work was designed to encourage independent thinking and objective judgment. Preference was given to those who had followed courses provided by extra-mural committees of universities, the Workers' Educational Association, Educational Settlements, and other adult organisations; and to those who had attended courses for adults organised by local education authorities. The college year consisted of three terms of ten weeks, roughly corresponding to university terms. The fees charged were £125 a year, but students had to find travelling expenses, books, and other personal expenses. The fees covered board, residence and tuition, and applied equally to men and women.

Newbattle was a masterpiece of beauty and design. The Abbey itself was founded by the Cistercians in 1140, and of their original building there still remains the beautiful Fratery with its vaulted roof and central row of columns. It stood like a jewel in its 125 acres of gardens, woodlands and parks. Lions crouched in stone above the pillars of the main gate. The drive led for almost half a mile through avenues of lofty trees to the handsome portico, and long before I entered the building I felt its atmosphere; as if the love of Edwin Muir and his wife Willa had already welcomed this stranger.

When I first saw Newbattle in the afternoon, the sun was shining. There were only a few people in the Abbey; it seemed so vast and empty – in the fine Italian gardens a few late blooms, the Esk glistering in the sun. I felt a bit sad and somewhat abandoned on that first day. Then Willa Muir took my hand, and led me under the great beech of Newbattle. Wife of the Warden, the poet and writer Dr Edwin Muir, and herself a writer and translator, she was almost aggressively eager to teach Latin or German to those students wishing to take languages.

'You have been a soldier,' said Willa. 'You will find peace here. Come, have some tea and heather honey.'

On my second day I was interviewed by the College secretary, Kenneth A. Wood, who advised me, as a trade unionist, to study Economics and Economic History – possibly because he taught those subjects – but to browse for a couple of days in the libraries, talk to other tutors and read the Curriculum before coming to a decision. On the third day, groping like the blind, I settled for Economics, Economic History, Political Theory, and English Literature. There were other subjects into which I was hurled later, but the curriculum was vast and, to me, at first sight most frightening.

English Language and English Literature were taught by Dr Muir, whose object was to foster a discriminating taste for and enjoyment of literature. His course began with a brief general account of English literature from Chaucer to the present day, after which a particular period or form could be selected for study. Lectures were given on the English language to train students to express their thoughts and feeling clearly and exactly. Kindly, tolerant, with an inexhaustible reserve of patience, Edwin's lectures, while of a high academic standard, were given with great clarity and simplicity. Because he was a fine poet, writer and literary critic, we thought we could not afford to miss one of his lectures, to be warned in his inimitable style against the atrocities we committed in everyday speech and writing upon the world's best language. We all plumped for English Literature.

Economics, to me a rather frightening subject, together with Economic History and Human Relations in Industry, was taught by Kenneth Wood, who possessed the knack of putting over the more difficult aspects of other people's theories so that even I could follow them. In spite of heavy tutorial and secretarial commitments he found time to give evening talks on Greek History and Greek Mythology, and to describe his own poems, some of which had been broadcast by the BBC. Because I was an ex-cavalryman, I committed one to memory.

CORINTH

Here below the fevered sun that grinds
Like a millstone on the dry brain
The crag of Acrocorinth hangs
Toothed with the ruins of the Frankish fort.
Only a few pariah dogs
Scamper among the columns,
The fallen capitals of the Roman shops,
Sharing Peirene with the droning bees.
Swifts hurtle from the upper air
And a sudden shadow falls as if
Great Pegasus again leapt forth, skyward,
Hoof striking spark and spring together
From the dry rock, for a moment
Wings blackening the sun. Or perhaps we hear
The shocked gasp that rose from the blockading Frank
When the Mace-bearer of later days
Enacting that fable once again
Proudly spurred his steed to the charge
And wingless soared from the battlements to fall
Where now the grapes lie spread
In rows, upon the hillside in the heat.

Kenneth explained to us that Pegasus, the winged horse of Bellerophon, Prince of Corinth, launching himself forth from the summit of Acrocorinth in an attempt to reach the skies, struck water from the dry rock, now called the Spring of Drakonera; and that in the year 1210 Leon Sgouros the mace-bearer, who held Acrocorinth for three years against the Franks, committed suicide by leaping astride his horse over the precipice, rather than surrender.

I liked Kenneth immensely. When the pony came to Newbattle I showed him how to mount it in cavalry style, and taught him how to give the constipated pony a pill by blowing one down its throat with a pea-shooter.

Miss Edith A. Lyle was the charming and beautiful lady who regaled us on the wickednesses of British and European History. Her subjects ranged from the Development of Western Civilisation to the political, social, ideological developments and international relations, and the impact of Western ideas on Asia and Africa. The special object of her course was to trace the origins and the course of the events which have shaped our own lives, and to understand the position of Britain and the Commonwealth in the present day. As if these were not big enough buns for us to get our teeth into, Miss Lyle taught evening classes in Appreciation of Music, and produced plays in which most of us took part.

My knowledge of radio came in handy when Edith Lyle produced 'Riders to the Sea'. When the windows and doors opened in that tragic cottage the sounds of the sea were the same as when they were closed. I managed to fix some spindles and pulleys to the drive of the volume control, and attached a drive cord to windows and doors. When they were opened, the effect was startling. Wind whistled at ear-shattering volume. Never before have the waves of the Irish Sea so volleyed and thundered.

George M. Brown, a fellow student from Stromness, now a poet of consequence and the winner of the Scottish Literary Award for his remarkable book, *An Orkney Tapestry*, wrote a speech for one of Edith Lyle's plays for our magazine, the *Sun*. And when I told him his words reminded me of the author at his best, 'wit-and-whisky-laden', he wrote a poem for me, 'The Pilgrim'.

What is this place I've come to now?
These are the perilous crossroads.
Here winds the peaceful road;
There the disgraceful road spins;
Now respectability highway;
But you turn to the path over the heather
That gleams like a sword.

What house is this the sun beats on?
Ah man, spurn these white walls.
The cat asleep on the broad sill,
The webbed ivy round the lintel
The deep rooms ringing with song,
And the sweet smells, blindly avoid.
(But he entered, and stayed the night.)

What man is that, gnarled like a tree?
He roves towards you, robed in all evil,
Rags on his shoulder, broken gums,
Naked feet twisted gravewards,
A drift of words from his heart's book.
Throw him a penny, pass quickly by.
'Old man, wait for me at the mile-stone.'

Night engulfs me. The dark torrent
Gurgles in my throat. Across my brain
Trek snarling winds of snow. O eyes,
Be patient, for this cannot last.
Soon wells of dawn will rinse the east,
A gull flashing, lounging around the sun,
The waves' fingers at their old embroidery.

Good angel, wholesome whisperer,
Are you with me still? . . .
Your road ends now

At the cliff's verge. Are you content?
The dark seas drum below you, the cold stars
Pierce you on three sides. I leave you here
For the mythical waves to gather or reject.
Cruel the path you choose, lucky your choosing.

Douglas R. Gordon like Kenneth Wood was married, and in a voice which compelled immediate attention he taught Philosophy, Political Theory, and Psychology. After the daily lectures he continued to give unstinted advice to perplexed would-be Existentialists in the quiet of his private chambers. This course covered a general statement of Philosophy with an initial account of current trends and with references back to Descartes and the British empiricists, Locke, Berkeley and Hume. There were protracted discussions on Moral Philosophy, with special reference to Hume, Kant, the English Utilitarians, and current linguistic theories of Ethics. There were more discussions on Logic, Scientific Method, Aesthetics and Philosophy of History. I thought Douglas Gordon was at his best on Political Theory. His great knowledge of Aristotle, Plato and Machiavelli was used to advantage when making comparison with current political practices and the ideas of Hobbes, Locke and Rousseau; but we were all sure that Douglas had a very weak spot for Mabbott. Psychology was in two parts: an historical introduction to Experimental Psychology, and the special problems of Social Psychology including the relationship to Child and Educational Psychology.

In addition to the set curriculum, special tuition was given to enable students to follow some particular line of work or research. Each student was required to write essays on his subjects, and individual tutorials were given in the friendly atmosphere of the tutor's private chambers. No punches were pulled in the criticisms, nor was there any lack of assistance. We were all impressed by the desire of the tutor to regard the student as his particular child – one who should be given the greatest attention at all costs, even to the curtailment of private leisure. Two days of the week were devoted to seminars, for which we were set a subject on which to write and then talk for half an hour. Views were torn to shreds in the subsequent free-for-all discussion – in which students and tutors took part in the liveliest way. This method proved invaluable in teaching us to think clearly, to put forward our views without undue nervousness, and experience us in the fast-declining art of self-expression.

Apart from the teaching, the catering was of a high standard, with a wide variety of well-cooked, wholesome food. Most students gained weight in the first week; but gymnastic facilities were available for the not-so-slim. Rooms were light and airy with plain but comfortable furniture and there were no petty restrictions. The whole atmosphere of Newbattle was tranquil and restful, conducive to thought and study, and friendly beyond belief; non-political, non-sectarian; but many a difference of opinion was aired during the winter months, around that glowing log fire in what we considered was the world's best debating chamber, the crypt, our common room, part of the original vaulted chamber built by the Cistercian monks in 1140.

We were a mixed bunch of twenty-four students of several nationalities and from all walks of life; clerks, fitters, tube-makers, turners, railwaymen, typists, journalists, teachers, civil servants. We were all eager beavers and wanted to learn, a fortunate minority of countless men and women scattered in jobs in all parts of the country with a bit of an intellectual passion or an undeveloped gift, which in most cases remains mis-shaped to their own misfortune and to the general loss. The students mostly came for a year, but there were exceptions. Some returned to their former work, others, like myself, went on to universities.

Gavin Muir, the son of Edwin, was not a student. He lived with his parents at Newbattle and took an active part in the cultural life of the college. As well as being an Honours graduate in Mathematics (St Andrews) he was a fine musician and spent most of his time practising and studying for a Mus. Bac. degree. Sometimes Gavin would take me to that large drawing room, sit down at the grand piano and pour out his friendship through the medium of my favourite piece, Claude Debussy's 'Clair de Lune'. It seemed to me more than a calamity when Gavin lost his hearing and had to forsake music.

But there were others at Newbattle who came with half-blinded wit, and left with full vision. Bob Fletcher was the classic example. He was a tube-maker whose only relaxation had been Saturday football matches and writing minutes for his trade union meetings on Fridays. During his second term he took a poem to Edwin Muir, saying: 'I dinna ken what my mates would say aboot this.' Edwin was delighted with Bob's new-found interest, and put pressure on him to return to college for a second year. He worked in his home town gas works for the summer vacation, returned to Newbattle and wrote an essay for the Cambridge Extra-Mural Delegacy. Later, he wrote one on *Paradise Lost*. Edwin sent it off. When the essay came back it was accompanied by the news that Bob had won a place at King's College. When I last heard of him he was teaching young Scots in the English department of a Scottish high school. His ability to put profundity of thought into the simplest of words was uncanny; but the poem about the drowning of Billy (we heard that Billy was his brother) sums up Bob's feeling.

ON THE DEATH OF BILLY BUDD

My God, since Billy's drowned you'd think the sea would
show some difference!
It should be higher, with a longer higher swell,
to account for that addition;
Or else a different shade, a different blending of
the grey and green,

To show that Billy's heart and brain have been dissolved.
But no, it looks the same to me,
It's still flip-flapping at the trippers' knees
And turning from the sand no later than
when Billy was alive.
And all that goodness, all that innocence and love,
all the seas,
Have all been drowned in that small sea.

Adrian Chadburn, our youngest student, was from Birmingham. He thrived on T. S. Eliot, wide open spaces, hitch-hiking and giving totally unwelcome and completely incomprehensible diatribes on Existentialism. These facets of his make-up could be readily detected in his peculiar paintings and drawings which he was so bold as to hang on the walls of the halls of Newbattle.

Margaret Darge was a teacher of music in Kilmarnock. It was a bit too much for her. Her heart was in bad shape when she came to Newbattle's peace to read Psychology and English Literature. She had several seizures, but we used to go in turns to her bedroom to deliver the lectures she had missed. George Innes thought up the bedroom lectures, it was just like him to do that, even though he was almost too shy to speak himself. Married, and an electrical engineer from Dundee, he was studying for entry into the Church, and walked Newbattle's Italian gardens in silence, with his Bible.

Blond, willowy and heavily bespectacled, David Stanton came from Nottingham, where he worked in a library. He was a tower of strength to Edith Lyle when she put on her plays, and constantly reminded us – when we butted in to suggest improvements – that there was only one producer. David studied Philosophy and English Literature and hoped to enter Birmingham University and eventually become a university librarian.

Vjera Starcevic, married, an Honours graduate of Belgrade

University, came at the beginning of the summer term to study English, which she already spoke better than most of us. She had worked in the Department of Foreign Affairs as an interpreter and had also taught English privately in Yugoslavia, and hoped to go on to Cambridge before returning to her home. She went to Cambridge. Although she could not face the plates of honest Scottish oats at our communal breakfast table, she left with us before she went a dissertation entitled 'Shakespeare on the Belgrade Stage (1945–1952)'. Belgrade had seen *Othello* in 1947, *Hamlet* in 1949, *As You Like It* in 1950, *Much Ado About Nothing* in 1951, and *King Lear* in 1952. Vjera wrote a summary of each play, and ended with these words:

'The unforgettable acting of the protagonists is one of the highest achievements of Yugoslav theatre art. The whole company succeeded in giving to the performance a thrilling inner monumentality, something deeply human, and all that in most simple expressions and beautifully spoken verses. The stage management was full of invention, skill and dexterity, so that the dreams of how to perform Shakespeare best came true. The five years of "groping" through five of Shakespeare's plays, brought at last a Shakespeare as he is: noble in thought, violent in judgment, and poetic in soul.'

Vjera was very poor. Her garments were threadbare and inferior. She said that her father, a lawyer, needed a month's pay to buy new boots. She had endured the German occupation, and the alleged improvements of Communism. She understood the richness of Shakespeare's words, but was baffled by the riches of common Scots. 'They all have such beautiful warm tweeds, Spike. They are all *allowed* to play golf!'

Tom Wilson did clerical work in Larbert. He was interested in poetry and English Literature and had achieved some success in short-story writing. At Newbattle he grew odd-looking beards and stayed in bed longer than most of us. Tom was convinced that somewhere outside, he did not specify where, he would find love and truth, if not work. Not that he was over-zealous about work.

Jimmy Jarvie had been a Grenadier in Hitler's war. He lived at Falkirk where in some iron foundry he churned cast metal into the shapes of common fire-grates. He had all the courage in the world, one would have thought, because he embarked upon poetry; we took Jimmy to task on his second endeavour:

THE MUSHROOM OF DEATH

I climb the hill and then look up
At the canopy of varied blue
And wonder.
Today you are smiling warmly
But tomorrow you may frown with a darkness
That will culminate in the ferocity of a storm
Jekyll and Hyde, unpredictable, unmerciful sky.
I see strange yet familiar patterns
Look! Greenland, Scylla and Charybdis,
And yonder is the mushroom of death
Suspended threateningly over the earth.
I see the face of Old Man Time himself,
Ever watching lest we escape retribution;
The price of being alive.

Spasmodically the poems and stories came in. Hither and thither moved the Muir wind of inspiration; here a new poem came to birth, and there a new story, passing from hand to hand round the crypt fire before being delivered to the typewriter or to the flames. Newbattle was a place of fierce but wholesome criticism. The undercurrent of gloom and despair in most of the contributions could not be put down to the atmosphere there, which was as happy and carefree as anywhere on earth; we were writing, I think, about the general gloom of the world outside which sometimes blew into our thick-walled fastness.

I had two firm friends in that place. Ragunath Chabria had taught English in Bombay University and was engaged in writing a book, *The Precocious Child in Victorian Fiction*, which later earned him his Ph.D. at Edinburgh. 'Chab' was barely five feet high. He had the fewest possessions. The blast of Scotland's east wind blew through his cotton jacket and pants to set his teeth all a-chatter. We called him the 'blue Indian', for he was usually blue with cold. Nevertheless, he was a most devout Hindu, and rose from his couch each dawn to go through the perishing process of total immersion in ice-cold water, to conform to the norm of his religious devotions. Chab had one suit, two pens, one *Concise Oxford Dictionary*, a sheaf of papers, and a heart as big as the Himalayas. We all loved him. He now looks after ineducable children in the Krishna Mission, Bombay, and writes to me once a year.

My other friend was Ettore Carinelli. I did not dream that one day I would be sitting in a private box at E.A. Teatro Alla Scala, Milan, listening to, for example, 'Aida', 'La Forza del Destino', 'La Traviata'; or that I would climb the towers of Citta di San Gimignano; or see Michelangelo's masterpiece 'The Last Judgment' on that immense wall of the Sistine Chapel; and see the work of Leonardo da Vinci and Raphael. It did not occur to me that I would ever wine and dine at the Biffi Scala and Giannino's, Milan, or stay in the best hotels throughout the length of sunny, hospitable Italy. But I did, several years running.

It was all on account (and on the account) of Ettore. Already a graduate from the universities of Rome and Milan, he had come to Newbattle Abbey College to ginger up his English. He had none. He became my room mate and we had trouble with 'communications'. I had no Italian. He spoke French with great fluency, and I had picked up a bit in Normandy. We got by. But within two months he got up on his hind legs at a seminar and spoke for a good twenty minutes, albeit with an atrocious accent, but in English, on the abstruse subject of the Division of Labour – he had been a parliamentary secretary in the Italian government and advised on Economic Affairs. He brought down the house. We always paid compliments to those who tried.

My trips to Italy were broached as we stood in Newbattle's great drawing room, admiring Van Dyck's portrait of Charles I.

'One day, Spike, you will come to Italy. I can show you better paintings, blue Italian skies, sunshine, good food and plenty of women.'

Ettore had been an officer in the Italian army. He had wealth and wit.

We were all Shakespeare mad. Tom Wilson set the ball rolling.

ON OPENING A NEW SHAKESPEARE

Compounded in the leaves were sects of woods
Of mouldering leaves of brackish heavy loam
Lost since page and forest, aye, Robin Hood's
With coloured plates like flames burning from
A bowl of incense held in clean-scrubbed hands,
Made rapturous senses struggle and beat
Like pegged white sheets heaving on hempen strands.
The motion of the words and memories sweet
Mingle like heady water lost in wine,
Marian and Juliet sip the full horn,
Mercutio, Friar Tuck and Falstaff dine.
The print has the tang of tar on a sharp morn
Brewed bubbling by witches in the cauldron night.
On nature poured in rhyme is the delight.

Poems poured forth, then Edwin Muir picked up his pen and put a stop to the deluge.

THE SHAKESPEAREAN HEROES

When they in all their bravery took the knock
And like obedient children swaddled and bound
Were borne to sleep deep in the chambered rock,
A splendour broke from that impervious ground.

Which they could never know. Whence came that greatness?
No fiery chariot wheeled them heavenwards, they
Saw no Elysium opening; but the straitness
Of full submission bound them where they lay.

What could that greatness be? It was not fame,
And yet they seemed to grow as they grew less,
And where they lay were more than where they had stood.
They did not go to any beatitude.
They were stripped clean of feature, presence, name,
When that strange glory broke from namelessness.

Edwin called me 'Spike the Practical'. I used to mend broken furniture, wireless sets, and make props for the plays. It was all good fun, but I proved the point about practicality at a seminar, when it was my turn to speak on any subject Edwin had lectured upon the week before. He had spent the best part of the week on the English Novel, and, on Daniel Defoe's *Robinson Crusoe*, he condemned repetitious and boring references to carpenter's tools – chisels in particular. I felt bound to go to Defoe's defence, saying it was all very well for Edwin to condemn a man who could use tools and write about men who could use them; that it would be more convincing if Edwin could use them. To my certain knowledge he could not knock a wire nail into a hunk of balsa wood without bending the nail, hammering his finger-nails, and splintering almost unsplinterable wood. Moreover, when he as a writer made some mistake, he had but to reach for an eraser and could then start again from scratch. Not so the chiseller. I invited Edwin's attention to the fireplace. Carved from one great tree was a massive grape vine, twelve feet wide and four feet high, bearing fruit and leaves. I asked Edwin to examine its detail, to note the curling fronds, the minute veins of the leaves and the beauty of the nodal joints. I reminded him that the Neapolitan carver had no eraser. One scratch, and his work was ruined. Edwin came and put his arm round me as Ettore thumped the table and drummed his mountaineering boots on the floor with delight. (Ettore always wore mountaineering boots.) As an afterthought, I added that more 'chiselling' was done on paper than on wood. Edwin took Carinelli and me to his study, and poured us sherry.

We gleaned much from the many lecturers and musicians who came to visit us, most of whom appreciated the informal nature of the talks round our crypt fire. J. Dover Wilson, the Shakespearean scholar, illustrated one of his talks with his own version of Shakespearean script on our blackboard. He referred to the passage in *Henry V* on the death of Falstaff which reads:

For his nose was as sharp as a pen
On a table of green fields.

With Professor Dover Wilson's emendation, out of apparent meaninglessness came

For his nose was as sharp as a pen
And a' babbled of green fields.

He went to lengths to explain that it was not a fountain pen . . . 'No, it was a quill pen; sharp and curved like Falstaff's beak. Oh, the clarity of Shakespeare's imagery!' Edwin Muir clapped him on the shoulder, thanked him for his refreshing gusto which he thought was of the Shakespearean kind, and said that Dover Wilson himself might well have stepped into our crypt straight from the period.

Edward Scouller gave talks on the structure of the short

story. Playwriting was the subject of Robert Kemp of the Scottish BBC who the year before had produced Lindsay's 'The Thrie Estaites' for the Edinburgh Festival. Talks were given by J. D. Scott on a new subject, 'The Literature of Despair'. Bubbling with mirth throughout, he was not all that convincing, so we had a good go at him. Walter Allen lectured on 'Contemporary Novelists'; and Norman McCaig and Alexander Scott, two young poets, spoke on the 'Lallans' poets.

Music was not neglected. An authority in the shape of Dr Hans Gal of Edinburgh University – an orchestra conductor in his native Austria between the wars, who was forced to flee from the Nazis – illustrated his theme by playing their music as he lectured on Haydn, Mozart, Beethoven and Schubert. Miss Jean Campbell, one of the few good clarsach players left in Scotland, accompanied herself on that instrument and sang in English and Gaelic – 'Leezy Lindsay', 'The Queen's Maries', 'Aignish on the Machair', 'Morag Bheag', and other songs. She had a wonderful voice, and the Scottish harp would have made St David turn in his Welsh grave.

Five Colonial students, travelling under the auspices of the British Council, who came from Nigeria, Tanganyika, Jamaica and Trinidad, delighted us one evening when they challenged us to a Brains Trust and licked the pants off us. The Trinidadian brought along records of his own calypso music, and we could have danced all night, and nearly did. His mind was brought to bear on the problems of Religion and Science when Professor John MacMurray who held the chair of Philosophy at Edinburgh lectured us near the end of term. I did not know that I would one day be sitting in one of his classes, as he tried to prove how a return to the principle of religious life could be used to solve most of the problems facing society today. I shall not forget his summing up, 'I am intellectually compelled to believe in God, and I am sure that most of you have found something of God here in Newbattle.'

Professor MacMurray was not far off the mark. I think we found bits of God in the weeks and months that followed. We sat round our crypt fire when the October evenings began to grow cold. Our eyes would flash as we argued over Science ('Its latest triumph is the atom bomb') and over religion. Two said 'dope for the masses'. But out of that came friendship, lasting friendship. On less tumultuous evenings, when quieter moods descended, we read poetry to each other. And, as the poet George Mackay Brown put it, 'If a man's voice trembled over a lovely line, we liked him the better for it.'

None of us will ever forget Saturday nights in the Justinlees – a corruption of 'Jousting Lees' – that little hostelry where five roads meet. Poetry takes on a richer meaning when there is a half empty glass of whisky in your hand, and you are with friends, and the eternal struggle between science and faith becomes a glorious joust. Our little earth is the arena. Stars in the Scottish skies, in their course, watch the outcome. No matter how passionate the argument, we could go together to our Abbey home, arm-in-arm, singing 'Steal Away', 'The Bonnie Wells o' Wearie', and always ending with 'The Lord is my Shepherd'.

The first autumn was golden, and lingered long. We knew ourselves on the fringes of winter only by the chill of the morning. Some students kept to their beds, until it was gently pointed out that it would be appreciated if we could see our way clear to getting up in the mornings.

The Abbey is haunted, of course, but the ghosts are kindly, and never trouble anyone. Old Webster, the caretaker, was an authority on them. One night he crept into the crypt when the rationalists had been getting the better of the argument (temporarily, of course) and began to tell us about the Grey Lady and the Grey Brother and the little spectral dog that brushes against one's arm on the spiral stair. It was said that no one dared sleep on the billiard table; but Jimmy Jarvie, being an ex-Grenadier, took on the bet. Just after midnight he returned to the crypt, ashen-faced and trembling. 'It's a' eerie cauld. There's somethin'. I dinna ken what it is!'

Then inexorable winter finally galloped upon us. We went to our separate homes for the Christmas vacation, and I was particularly glad to return three weeks later. I had tried to get a temporary job during this vacation because funds were low, and applied to London (Heathrow) Airport, about three miles from my home. My particulars were taken by a female personnel manager who placed me in her card index file as a 'student'.

'We are Fortes, the caterers. We deal with food. You will have to be medically examined before we take you on. Take this letter to the doctor and bring it back to the main restaurant tomorrow.'

I returned next day, in my best suit. The catering manager ushered me into the main restaurant on the North Side. I said I was about to take over a job there. He brought me coffee and biscuits before the personnel manager came to see my letter and the medical certificate.

'Oh yes, we have a job for you, as a plateman.' She led me to a kitchen, piled with greasy plates. Disgusting portions of vegetable and animal matter swirled in the grease-topped water of a filthy sink. A little man with misery eyes was in that water, up to his armpits. He did not smell as sweet as my medical certificate.

'Can you start tomorrow? If you start now it will spoil our wages system.'

I went home and told young John I had got a job, as a plateman, and gave him the details.

'Oh, no, Dad . . . don't go . . . I can't bear it!'

I did not go. Instead, I helped out in a little sub-Post Office.

No one will ever know how glad I was to get back to Newbattle Abbey, to escape from exploitation, from the illusory and commercial revelries of Christmas and New Year; to be back inside those sturdy walls which made the outside world seem remote, unnecessary and unreal. They all had tales to tell, not unlike mine, before we returned to our books.

One cold January morning, after a night of storm, Adrian Chadburn burst breathlessly into bedrooms to announce that Newbattle's 400-year old beech, the pride of the parish, had fallen. George Mackay Brown ticked him off, and said it was a joke in bad taste. But Adrian was right. The great tree whose branches had reached down to earth had fallen. All that day, and for many following, little knots of people gathered in the slush to gaze sorrowfully at the stricken colossus. Everyone felt it to be symbolic, though of what nobody knew.

Edwin and Willa Muir were much upset, and we were upset for them. It was always a revelation to see them together hand-in-hand under that tree, with love in their eyes. After that day, they walked in the gardens.

My second term was notable for the failure of the heating. Suddenly the vast building went as cold as charity, and stayed that way for a fortnight. Morning ablutions were painful – quick splashes and shudders; frenzied gropings for the towel. Shaving, though almost impossible, was manfully accomplished out of consideration for the ladies. But the bitter cup was not yet full; hard frost set in and the snow came. Overnight the landscape became blank, except for bastions of black, sombre trees. Day after day students set forth with axes, frosted breath and glowing faces – to hew logs for the crypt fire. Every night after dinner there were fierce, mute struggles for the best armchairs, nearest to the blazing logs. Not a single concession was made for sex or infirmity. For two weeks life was a relentless struggle for heat.

What joy there was when the boiler was mended! That Monday afternoon when we felt the warmth flowing from heaters into hands, most of us fled into baths, and wallowed for hours in a lotus dream. Hearts thawed. Brains thawed. Chadburn rhapsodised about existentialism to anyone who would listen, and arranged his second art exhibition on the walls of his bedroom. Bob Fletcher extolled Herman Melville and Blake; Bill Drysdale put in several thousand words on behalf of Keats and Shelley; Jimmy Jarvie wrote dashing impromptu poems with one hand and enthusiastic essays with the other. And from the drawing room at dimmit light stole the melodies of Beethoven and Chopin; Gavin Muir was at his beloved piano to tell us that Newbattle's brief but bitter winter had been banished.

We continued to write poems, plays, stories, essays, and letters home. On Sunday evenings, gramophone recitals. On alternate Monday evenings, play reading – the 'Antigone' of Sophocles, 'The Moon in the Yellow River', 'Campbell of Kilmhor', 'The Doctor's Dilemma'. We took our various parts in three one-act plays for the end of the session.

After the Easter vacation – and a spell of licking stamps at Feltham sub-Post Office – spring was breaking out all over. Trees budded and shook out their tender leaves under the sun like myriads of small green lanterns. Gold and purple crocuses faded from the banks of the Esk, to make way for daffodils and anemones. Magnolias stood on their branches like stiff white candles against the Abbey's south wall. And throughout the third term deputy managers from the National Coal Board came to study. They came in batches of thirty for a week's course. At first we received them in some trepidation, but soon relations could not have been more cordial; especially on Thursdays, when the deputies' party was held in the crypt, and we danced and sang together long into the night.

Edwin Muir asked me to his study about a month before my course was due to end.

'Sit down, Spike. I have a proposition to put to you. You have a love and natural aptitude for study, and should go on to university. If you can persuade the GPO to give you leave for another two years, I will recommend you for Social Study at Edinburgh.'

My application for further leave (and an educational grant)

was in the post within the hour. A week later the reply stated I could have two years leave (unpaid). My seniority and entitlement to pension would remain unimpaired, but a grant was out of the question. Edwin Muir came to my aid by writing a strong recommendation to the Middlesex County Council. Next day I attended the Department of Social Study, University of Edinburgh, where Dr Gregor, a most charming lady, asked many questions, then said that if I was successful at my London interview she would accept me as a student. I was truly delighted.

In No. 10 Great George Street, Westminster, I met C. E. Gurr, the Chief Education Officer and Secretary to the Education Committee of Middlesex. Seated with him behind a shiny table were other studious-looking gentlemen. Starting from the left flank they in turn asked me many questions. After rounding the course about four times, the Chairman popped the sixty-four thousand dollar question.

'Do you think that at your age you will be able to assimilate all the knowledge that is required in this course of eleven subjects, Mr Mays?'

I hesitated, then took the plunge.

'I do not wish to be discourteous, but it appears that you are all senior to me in age, gentlemen. May I suggest that the young ones be given a chance?'

Nary a blink, smile or hint came from those imperturbable inquisitors.

'Thank you, Mr Mays,' said Mr Gurr. 'That will be all. We will write to you!'

Lead was light compared with the heaviness of my heart. Sorrowfully I went home to Vera, to say I had muffed it. Next morning I telephoned Dr Muir; to tell him the sad tidings, to apologise for letting him down. But Edwin was jubilant.

'Congratulations, Spike! You've pulled if off. Did you actually call them old fogies? Never mind. They have granted you a Major County Award. I think it's £300 a year. You are all set for Edinburgh. Well done!'

I returned to Newbattle to finish my course, in a whirl of dreams. But down in the bushgrowth of the Scottish Department of Education unpleasant things were astir. From the Executive Committee Dr Muir learned that the Scottish Department of Education was profoundly concerned about the college's finances. Unless more students were enrolled it might have to be closed. Letters appeared in the *Scotsman*, including an appeal by Lord Lothian. I read this with great distress. On 20 October 1952 I wrote to the *Scotsman*.

Sir,

Allow a grateful Englishman, who has spent one profitable year at Newbattle Abbey College, heartily to support its continuance as a successful and highly efficient institution for adult education.

I endorse every word written in its favour by your previous correspondents and condemn the evasive insinuations which were made in the speech of that gentleman who, by virtue of his office, should have been better informed.

He may be interested to learn that, apart from the high standard of academic tuition given by the resident tutorial staff of Newbattle, lectures are also given there by Professor John MacMurray, Professor Sir Alexander Gray, Mr Neil Gunn, Professor Dover Wilson, Mr Duncan Macrae, and renowned scholars from the University of Edinburgh. Unlike the first critic, these gentlemen are of the opinion that Newbattle is doing a pretty good job. . . .

As a result of their training at Newbattle, 1951–2, five students have obtained scholarships to the universities of Cambridge and Edinburgh.

The Marquess of Lothian has appealed, through your columns, for the support of this College in a difficult period of its history. A better example could be set by those who hold office and profess to be interested in the departments of Scottish educational administration.

The tutorial staff of Newbattle Abbey College have made it possible for this ex-professional soldier with 20 years service to know the University of your City from the inside.

Thank you, Newbattle.

I am, &c. C. W. Mays.

My letter was published, and more besides, and I am very glad to say that the College was saved and continues its good work. Quite recently I recommended a young friend of mine to Newbattle and was delighted to learn that the new Warden had accepted him as readily as the University of Edinburgh accepted me after a warm recommendation from Edwin Muir. I am equally sure that my old friend George Mackay Brown was pleased to learn that Newbattle survives. I have a copy of the words he wrote about our Abbey just before we departed.

For most of us the future is a large cheerful question mark. Whatever happens, we will never forget our happy terms at Newbattle Abbey College. Perhaps, hunched rheumatically over the fire on a winter's night, we will tell our grandchildren of a place . . .

'Where falls not rain, nor hail, nor any snow
Nor ever wind blows loudly; but it lies
Deep meadowed, happy, fair with velvet lawns
and bowery hollows.'

Not a strictly accurate picture, of course. But imagination has her own truths, and this is one of them. Although not yet rheumatically hunched, I have told my own grandchildren.

SEVENTEEN

Edinburgh University

Thy sons, Edina, social, kind,
  With open arms the stranger hail;
Their views enlarg'd their liberal mind,
  Above the narrow, rural vale:
Attentive still to Sorrow's wail,
  Or modest Merit's silent claim;
And never may their sources fail!
  And never Envy blot their name.

Robert Burns

I WAS troubled. Whether I should proceed to a place of learning and cram myself with culture, or resume soul-destroying work to put food into my son John's belly in the hope that he one day might go to university? That was the question. There were two quick answers.

'You go, Dad,' said John. 'You have tried hard.'

'You MUST go, Cedric,' said Vera. 'I'll work at the factory full time.'

I was glad, and yet sorry, and decided to go.

A month before, I had read in *The Times* W. E. Styler's criticism of a lecture by A. L. Rowse which had appeared in the paper. Styler agreed and disagreed with Rowse's postulation, 'Equality does not mean mediocrity', and specified in detail two different kinds of life, the normal, and the intellectual. It appeared that the normal was that of the undergraduate who played all the games, dressed in the right uniform, got pickled, chased the women, and did as much or as little work as necessary to remain at the university. The other life was of the cultivated man, who read hard, attended all the debating societies and concerts, concerned himself with art, philosophy and politics, and availed himself to the full of the opportunities universities had to offer.

For his statistical analysis Styler chose Oxford, where, over a period of ten years, the relative percentages of undergraduates in the two classes scarcely varied, 'even when Oxford was wholly aristocratic, largely middle-class and almost half working class'. C. E. M. Joad also crept into the act, and into the columns, and extracts were quoted from his *Culture and the Community*, in which he attempts to distinguish between equality and inequality where education is concerned.

I felt bound to write to *The Times* agreeing with Professor Joad's statement that what is more important than any abortive attempt to prove something by statistics is that every man and woman should be given the chance of showing whether he or she is an intellectual or not. Joad stressed that opportunities were equal for the normal and the intellectual at these places of learning. But there equality ended. There were two intellectual ladders, each with rungs. That of the privileged had the most rungs – nursery, governess, kindergarten, preparatory school, public school, and university. The second ladder had only two rungs – elementary school, and (by scholarship) grammar school.

On leaving the top rung of the first ladder (possibly at the age of twenty-three or twenty-four) the doors of all professions and the windows of all cultures gaped wide. The second educational ladder had but one rung for me. At the age of twelve the doors were open wide to clod-hopping and shoe-cleaning.

But I was not unduly dissatisfied with my lot. Grandfather Reuben Ford had given me a tip or two on those rare occasions when he broke into speech – usually after he had downed a few pints in celebration of a good harvest.

'All yer want in life is trust in God, a sharp shut-knife, a shillun, a whistle, an' a bit o' string.'

'What's the string for?'

'Ter tie up yer trap when yer arsk silly questions.'

Possibly because I could always respond to those pleasant fields and woodlands where natural beauty reigned, and to what little I knew of art and literature, I thought there should be more to life than that. Even after I had become coarsened by military life, my innate appreciation was not impaired, and it occurred to me that it might be improved. With precious memories of Newbattle Abbey flaming in my head, and new books in my cardboard suitcase, I moved off to Edinburgh, not to a dingy barrack room at Colinton, but to civvy digs at No. 1 Leamington Terrace. A new life was about to dawn.

Mrs Shaw looked after me. There was a lot of her. She bulged and wheezed and was forever puffing up her wispy fringe by blowing hard on her underlip, a kind of cooling process because at the slightest exertion she would break out in muck sweats. She did not speak, she gasped, and fed the pair of us – Joe Fraser and me – like fighting cocks. There were just the two of us there at first. Joe was a fifth-year veterinary student who loved whisky, a nurse from Edinburgh Infirmary, and most of all, study. Like myself, Joe had come up the hard way. We had much in common, apart from the language, and shared a room. Day after day he made me almost collapse with helpless laughter, telling me extraordinary stories about the behaviour of his fellow students at the Royal Dick Veterinary College.

Miss Marjorie M. Brown, the Director of Social Studies, was the first of the university staff to greet me. My fears were dispelled within minutes.

'You have read a lot of books, Mr Mays. If you can remember what you have read you will get by. But it is a tough and crammed course. If you get into difficulties, just come and tell me. I am here to help you.'

Truer words were never spoken!

Next day I paid £2 12*s* 6*d* matriculation fee, and was given Card No. 1165 on which was printed – to my great joy:

> Note: This card, which the Applicant receives when Matriculation Fee of Two and One-half Guineas has been paid or is under claim from a Grant-giving Authority, entitles him to present himself for enrolment in one or more of the University Classes, and thus to obtain all the privileges of Studentship.

I could have turned cartwheels, but was brought back to my deplorable ignorance by the red overprinting on my card . . . *Civis Edinburgensis a Kalendis Octobribus* MCMLII. It conveyed nothing.

I underwent the probing eyes of the mass-miniature-radiography to determine if T.B. was present. It was a bit different from the military short-arm inspections, where we all had to strip to the buff. Towels were supplied to cloak our upper nudity, as we waited in long queues, male and female alike.

Jane Allison, a fellow student-to-be on her post-graduate course, handed me a nerve-shattering catalogue and the reading list required for my studies.

In the afternoon I made a swift reconnaissance of the University Library, then took a long walk over the Pentland Hills. I looked down on Redford Barracks and thought of Sgt Doughy Baker, my musketry instructor in the Royal Dragoons, and his words . . .

'On the command "load", you gets dahn to it!'

And when I looked at the timetable for the autumn term, I realised I had to get down to it again.

a.m.	*Mon.*	*Tues.*	*Wed.*	*Thurs.*	*Fri.*
10.0	Social Philosophy	Social Philosophy (Tutorial)	Social Philosophy	Social Philosophy (Tutorial)	Social Philosophy
11.0	Psychology	Psychology (Statistics)	Psychology	Psychology (Statistics)	Psychology

p.m.	*Mon.*	*Tues.*	*Wed.*	*Thurs.*	*Fri.*
2.0	Social Philosophy	Youth Employment (Practical)	Psychology	Youth Employment (Practical)	Psychology
3.0	Psychology (Statistics)	Youth Employment (Practical)	Psychology	Youth Employment (Practical)	Social Philosophy
annexe 9.0 *a.m.*	Political Economy	Political Economy	Economic History	Economic History	Political Economy
12 *noon*	Discussion: Miss M. Brown. 'Social Case Work'				

My first lecture did not conform to the timetable, because the subject was not Political Economy. It was a kind of welcome or introduction, perhaps the highlight of my life. Although I was present with swarms of young students I felt a bit out of place, a usurper, as we sat together in the magnificent Pollock Hall. Then, from the door at the left of the massive organ came a slight grey-haired, middle-aged gentleman who walked briskly to his rostrum, pushed up his spectacles to his forehead and took a sip of water as his eyes roved over his assembled flock.

'Good morning, ladies and gentlemen! From this place I have talked to your parents, to their parents and to others before them. Some describe me as a mid-Victorian; others regard me as a late-Edwardian. I am merely your tutor in Economics, and am delighted to meet you.'

With these words Sir Alexander Gray, the Professor of Commercial and Political Economy, introduced himself before galloping like a good Scots Grey on a lightning introduction to his own textbook, *The Development of Economic Doctrine.* I glanced down at the copy in my hand which I had bought after leaving Newbattle, and wondered if ever I would begin to understand this strange language . . .

The industrious gleaner may therefore collect from the oldest literature chance observations and stray remarks which the enthusiast may hail as containing in the embryo a doctrine of Adam Smith or the kernel of the philosophy of the Physiocrats. Apart from the obiter dicta of poets and philosophers, all customs, institutions and laws much contain implicitly a certain measure of economic theory, even if it be never expressly propounded. An Act which forbids usury involves a denial of the legitimacy of interest, and inferentially an affirmation of the barrenness of money. . . .

And when the professor had finished plugging his book, he began to tease us by asking riddles . . . perhaps to cheer us.

'What is the difference between a pig hanging in a butcher's shop and a student of Economics?' The reply was stony silence. No one dared to hazard a guess. But we were enlightened.

'Apart from the lemon in the pig's mouth, there is usually an expression of intelligence upon its face.' Roars of laughter.

'What is the difference between mortar boards as carried by bricklayers and those worn by graduates?' Silence reigned.

'When carried by bricklayers mortar boards have cement on top. When worn by graduates they have concrete underneath.'

Pollock Hall rocked with appreciative laughter. I had the feeling that we all felt we could put up with 'Alec' Gray, who then asked us to question him on any subject. A bedworthy blonde from Washington D.C. asked, 'Say, Professor, whatdyer think of ballroom dancing?'

'I am glad you asked. It is but a vertical expression of a horizontal desire. Learn the Dashing White Sergeant. Next question?' So it went on.

With my brain buzzing like Walton's Park beehives, I raced to another room for the 10.0 a.m. lecture on Social Philosophy; but I had got my map reference wrong and found myself seated for a lecture on Psychology, where a young tutor, all bible-black gowned and earnest looking introduced a list of what he called 'set books'. 'You can buy them all at Ferrier's,

Teviot Place.' The cheapest was 25*s*. I wondered if he held shares in Ferrier's, and in my state of economic ill-health I had to settle for Stafford Clarke's *Psychology* (Pelican Series, 3*s*).

Professor Drever arrived. For years his father had held the Chair of Psychology at Edinburgh. It was rumoured that he succeeded in following his father's footsteps on grounds of Scottish thrift. The Senatus Academicus did not have to pay out bawbees for a new name to be painted on the door. Drever the Younger was a most handsome man, with a voice like a missel-thrush and an excellent memory. Without notes, for he had none, he pierced us with probative eyes as he delivered his introduction.

> Psychology has much in common with biology (the science of life) and sociology (the science of social phenomena). It is indeed both a biological (natural) and a social science. Nevertheless, the interests of psychologists in living things and in social functions are more restricted and have a somewhat different emphasis from those of biologists and sociologists . . .

The words frightened the living daylights out of me and I began to wonder what I had let myself in for. Some of the problems were ironed out in the Common Room, where students congregated after lectures for bridge-playing, coffee and conversation. The young were most willing to help one so old in the tooth, and after the first week I began to get the hang of it.

More help came from my digs in Leamington Terrace from three young gentlemen who came to live with us and were reading Medicine, Clive Hinwood, Hamish MacDonald, and John Yeoman, a graduate of Oxford. Because I was a bit thin on top, they christened me 'Curly', and in the presence of ladies they addressed me as 'Professor Skinheid'. With their help I got a mental picture of what was happening. Though at first the subjects seemed extremely diverse, with each professor specialising in his own field, I began to appreciate how closely those seemingly dissimilar subjects were integrated. The magic casement had begun to open.

Between them Marjorie Brown, the Director of Social Studies, and Dr Gregor covered a vast field: Family Casework, Medical Social Work, Psychiatric Social Work, Probation Work, Child Care, Boarding-out Officers; and continued with the after-war problems which challenged the Statutory and Voluntary social services alike. These two ladies knew their subjects, but not only from textbooks. They had been practical case-workers and had given aid to stricken families in some of the surliest slums of Britain. They did not enter those hovels with words and pamphlets, but with their sleeves rolled up, brooms and scrubbing brushes at the high port, and with pens and papers to instruct the incapable on how to balance their meagre budgets. When we heard them recounting their experiences of filth and squalor and human misery, we thought it almost incredible that such cultured 'gentle' ladies had that capacity. Bill Townsend penned an ode about one of them.

> Listening here tae Maggie Broon,
> Wrapit in her scholar's goon,
> I would ha'e bet a quid, or mair,
> She'd noo the spunk tae scrub a flair.

Taught by a team of youngish men and women under the guidance of Professor Norman Hunt, Organisation of Industry and Commerce was not the dry-bone subject I feared it might be. Because I had been active in trade unions for several years, I found the course revealing and quite fascinating. The accent was upon the recognition of workers as human beings; as 'persons', and not as 'hands', or other soulless terms of identification. I remember Norman Hunt's words, 'Let each worker know how he is progressing. Give him credit when it is due. Tell people in advance about changes that will affect them, and why. Look for ability not being used. Treat them as individuals, not as numbers on a wages sheet.'

Many nations were represented in this class, but there was one Scot of great consequence, David Bell. Once charred almost to a cinder, still war-blinded, with artificial arms and legs, David was gently guided to his place each day by many willing hands. I was deeply moved and inspired by his courage which, later, was made the subject of a television programme in the series 'This is Your Life'.

My practical work included one term (three half days a week) with the Ministry of Labour; three weeks with the Probation Department at Uxbridge; one term with the Youth Employment Officer, Edinburgh; four weeks in the Personnel Department of Horlicks Ltd, Slough; one term with the National Assistance Board; and four weeks with the Personnel Department of Glaxo at Greenford.

It was extremely interesting and enlightening, and not without humour. I had to deal practically with some of the problems of delinquent children in the Youth Employment Section of the Ministry of Labour and National Service. Some of the experiences were dramatic, tragic in a few cases, but one humorous incident stands out in my mind to temper a bit of the drama.

One lad had been placed on probation for petty larceny. His mother went out early to work and the lad used to stay in bed until midday. To pass away the afternoon he would collect various articles from the counters of multiple stores, to sell. He was granted probation on the understanding that the Youth Employment Officer would find him a job which got him early from his bed. A job was found . . . milkman's assistant. Never had there been an earlier riser, a more conscientious deliverer of milk. He also fed and groomed the horse, washed the dirty milk bottles, and whistled merrily as he took each bottle to each doorstep. Congratulatory letters were sent to the Youth Employment Office on its remarkable ability to assess human worth. But one day the lad got up earlier than usual and went round on his own. It was Friday – pay day. He collected all the money, and has not been seen since.

Another lad appeared before the Sheriff's Court. With an air gun and a box of fifty pellets, he had shot out all the light bulbs down the Royal Mile leading to Holyrood Palace. His excuse was that he wanted to be a 'sodger'. His wish was granted, and he enlisted on boy service.

Two other lads had engaged in an unusual form of racketeering. In the tail end of October and the beginning of November, they had systematically robbed children of the pennies they collected for the Guy on 5 November.

At the Port of Leith we were shown over great ships and warehouses, and were told stories of alcoholics who drank the biddy and methylated spirits, and of one enterprising sailor who broke open ship's compasses to drink the spirit. Later, we had to meet them and try to reform them, but most were too far gone to care.

My month at Horlicks of Slough was instructive. One of my jobs was to interview applicants for various jobs, and for a fortnight I did little else and became attached to the Personnel Department.

A telephone call came from the Publicity Manager the day before I was due to leave. 'You must come and see us before you go.' I am glad I went.

The Publicity Manager showed me round his emporium, introduced me to his methods, gave me a solemn warning about the perils of advertising, and stressed that 'ambiguity' had to be avoided at all costs. He gave a classic example of failure. At the time, Horlicks were advertising by strip cartoon. In the first picture there was shown a haggard, woebegone, weedy individual, stripped to the waist, as a doctor puggled his bosom with a stethoscope. In picture two the doctor burst into speech, 'There is nothing organically wrong with you. All you need is sound, refreshing sleep. You must take Horlicks.' In picture three the scene changed. In a fish queue a starry-eyed housewife was boasting to her fellow queuers . . . 'Since my husband has been taking Horlicks he has had three rises in a month!'

'Now, Mr Mays,' said the Publicity Manager, 'who would have thought those pictures had the content of ambiguity? I certainly did not. At least not until we received a letter from a retired colonel at Cheltenham. His letter ran something like this: "Since reading your advertisement I have been taking your product with monotonous regularity, but without result. Kindly state if the rises referred to were financial or biological."'

In my second vacation arrangements were made for me to take a course of practical training in Personnel Management under the kindly and efficient auspices of Glaxo. The company had an industrious team in their widening field of scientific personnel management, and through their activities a relationship between employer and employed had been produced, based on friendship, understanding, tolerance and mutual co-operation. Functioning strictly on a 44-hour week, there was no overtime. Shift-working was confined to departments where alternative systems were impracticable. In the event of a workman being called in for some emergency task outside normal hours, he would be compensated by time off at some date to suit him. There were sports grounds to which the company contributed substantially, and a Sports and Social Club provided employees with facilities for indoor and outdoor sporting and social events; the canteen meals were excellent, and were reasonably priced. Arrangements existed for staff to buy the company's products at reduced prices. To safeguard the health of the staff, a medical officer, dentist and nurse were in constant attendance. The mental aspect had not been disregarded. Leave of absence was granted to allow staff to attend educational courses – during paid working hours – at technical or commercial schools, or professional institutes. This scheme provided financial assistance towards fees, books, instruments and fares; and the Personnel Department was always eager to advise on suitable courses, and how to apply for assistance.

I could not help but reflect upon the benevolence of the GPO. It was not all beer and skittles for me at Edinburgh University. Cash was always short with two homes to keep, but I managed to eke things out peeling spuds at half a crown a sack for the fish and chip saloons at Dalkeith; by sweeping out rail coaches at Waverley and Princes Street Stations, and washing dishes in hotels. My wardrobe consisted of one de-mob suit, one blazer and a pair of flannels. Of course I had shoes and socks and shirts, but I lashed out a month's spud-bashing money on what economists describe as 'conspicuous consumption'. I bought for myself – with great pride – one tie, one blazer badge, one scarf in the colours of Edinburgh University. I felt that at last I had arrived. Whether or not I should pass had still to be determined by examination.

In the second term I was elected Secretary to the Social Study Society and to the Students' Representative Council. This was a different kind of trade unionism from the GPO. No squawks about exploitation, no rebels, and, unlike today, no posters and take-over bids. We had about a dozen level-headed dedicated young folk doing their best to help not only their colleagues and the tutorial staff, but unfortunate folk outside the university. We formed committees, hired top-flight entertainers and artistes to perform in Edinburgh's cinemas and theatres; and on Annual Rag Day collected a great deal of money for the cancer research campaign.

It was a great day for us when the Duke of Edinburgh was installed as Chancellor; to entertain him in the Common Room, and to see him chatting merrily to doll-like maidens from Malaya, and to learned gentlemen like Sir Alexander Fleming, of penicillin fame. Each Sunday some members of the Students' Representative Council attended matins in St

Giles's Cathedral. I found it a moving experience to go to the robing room and put on Edinburgh's red toga before sitting in stalls near the altar next to that magnificent mixed choir. My mind took me back to All Saints', Ashdon, and the time when the Reverend Hartley had publicly rebuked two boy choristers, brother Leslie and myself, for laughing aloud during a hymn at the dithering of Starchy Williams's oscillating Adam's apple. But ever accident-prone, I put a foot wrong on my first attendance at St Giles. Two black velvet collecting bags had been placed in my hand as I left the robing room. I was appointed a collecting point, but was given no further instructions. Just before the beginning of the recessional hymn, we moved to our positions. At All Saints', Ashdon, it was the custom to start garnering the financial sheaves the minute the organist's fingers touched the keys for the introductory bars. It was different at St Giles's Cathedral. I should have waited for the beginning of the last verse. Instead, I pushed my bags under the noses of outraged Scots at the first note of the first verse. Like nests of cobras from the banks of Mother Ganges there came from the banks of the aisles great hissings of clerics and congregation. There were nods and pointings towards my fellow collectors, all indicating that unlike me they had remained static. One of the professors approached me as I was removing my toga in the vestry. 'You got your inspiration to collect a little early in the service, Mr Mays.' I reminded him that I was English, a student of Economics and Time and Motion Study, and thought it advisable to catch as many Scots as possible – in case they sneaked out. The professor was not amused.

Being English had some advantages. One pleased me enormously, for I could put my feet where the feet of Scots could not tread; as a 'foreigner', I was entitled to join International House, a fine club in Princes Street, and was permitted to enter for the international chess tournament – the only representative of Merrie England. I was victorious over French, Spanish and

Italian players, but in the semi-finals was defeated by a cunning Pole from Warsaw.

Another foot was put wrong when I arranged for a party of Social Study students to visit the coal mines of nearby Gilmerton. Most were young ladies who wore stout shoes and carried walking-sticks and compasses, because my notice had said the going might be hard and stragglers might get lost in the dark burrows. The Mine Manager was a man of understanding. As we entered the cage for the descent, I told him that my young ladies had never been down a mine before, so would he let the cage down gently. I gave him a wink. The cage was dropped like a stone, and gave the girls a bit of a thrill. Not quite such a good one as they received later. After we had de-caged at the end of our inspection, coal-grimed of face and hands, I said, 'Come with me. We will go to the miners' baths and wash.' The minute we entered the door there emerged from a shower a great hunk of ginger-maned miner, as naked as he was born. Only the miner was really embarrassed.

Coming down for the summer vacation in 1953 I took a train from Waverley Station. In an otherwise empty compartment I found a discarded copy of the Dundee newspaper the *Weekly News*. Between pictures of bulging buttocks and mammoth mammory glands was a rip-snorting article – one of a series of five – on Colonel A. D. Wintle's release from Fort Ste Catherine, Toulon, in Occupied France, during the war. No reference was made to his death, although I had been told he was shot while trying to escape, but there was a footnote to say the article was an extract from 'It is an Offence to Duck', a new book by Wintle, shortly to be published (it was never published). Delighted to discover that he might still be alive, I wrote to the editor for confirmation of his survival and his address, and added that he had once saved my life – way back in 1924. By return of post I received a reply from the editor, which gave Wintle's address, confirmed that he was living there, and asked me to send an article on how Wintle had saved my life. I thought I would get Wintle's permission first, and wrote to him to say I hoped he was alive, and that I was reading Economics and Psychology at Edinburgh. The reply came by return of post.

COLDHARBOUR
Wrotham
Kent

Dear Mays,

I am delighted to hear from you. Yes, I am still alive. Life remains uneventful. I am still writing a good deal, but not as much as I wish, there are complications.

You surprise me by your confession that you are trying to unravel the mysteries of Economics and Psychology – I had thought you to be intelligent.

From what I know of these subjects there is little mystery attached to either. Economics is a bastard science, whose terminology has been designed to make the obvious appear difficult. Among its many definitions is one attributed to the London School of Economics, 'The Science of Wealth'.

Professors of this dubious science are prepared to eke out a meagre existence in dingy garrets; content to receive two guineas a month for a series of interminable, incomprehensible lectures. If I lectured on 'The Science of Wealth' it would be from my diamond-encrusted yacht, moored off Monte Carlo.

As for Psychology, it merely consists of telling people to stop dying and get their hair cut. You should know about that.

A good place to find me is the Bull Hotel, Wrotham. Make it 12 noon on Thursday. Your luncheon will be poured in readiness.

A. D. Wintle.

Due to the unpredictable capers of British Railways, I was late on parade. Wintle had just taken a prodigious pinch of snuff and was adjusting his eye-glass.

'You are two minutes late, Mays. That is not the form of the Royal Dragoons. Whisky?'

We shook hands and took stock. At fifty-seven years of age I had expected him to look a bit war-worn. He was not. His wicked eye roved round as if he expected or suspected that enemies lurked everywhere. His shoes shone like patent leather. I could see he still cleaned them himself because the arch between sole and heel was carefully polished. Not a speck of dust was in his turn-ups. He wore the tie of the Royals. I assumed all was well.

During a delightful afternoon of military reminiscing in his half-timbered fourteenth-century farmhouse in the Kentish Wold, he confided that all was not well. Some solicitor had deprived his sister Marjorie of her rightful inheritance by making his client's Will in his own favour.

'I have gone to great lengths to expose the scoundrel, but with little success. You may rest assured, Mays, that although the authorities are reluctant to move, I am not. I shall be attending to this solicitor very shortly, and I may need your help.'

We left it at that, but I did not suspect that one day I would be involved in a legal battle which would hit the national headlines after eleven years of litigation, culminating in the House of Lords.

The Hayes Post Office was as reluctant to move as Wintle's 'authorities', and declined to employ me during my vacation...

'You see, Mr Mays, you are on leave for two years. We had to fill your vacancy and cannot be over-borne.'

From time to time, and from place to place, I found odd jobs to keep the flag flying, and continued to study for the term to come. Apart from leaving my wife and son, I was glad to return to the friendly world of Edinburgh.

Joe Fraser cheered me when I arrived back at our digs in Leamington Terrace. He and the Medics had been having high jinks during the absence of Professor Skinheid, the controlling element. After one night of celebration in the Golf Tavern they discovered that a sixpence would fit the brass screws pinning nameplates to the walls of doctors, dentists, solicitors and other professional folk who dwelt in splendour not far from Leamington Terrace. In no time at all they switched the name-plates, causing solicitors to refuse to extract teeth, and doctors to refuse to accept legal briefs. The following night, in celebration of this enterprise, they had knocked at the door of a stately house in Craiglockhart and begged the loan of a handsaw.

'There have been complaints about an ugly tree growing in this locality and we have been ordered by the Department of Health to cut it down.'

The lady of the house provided the saw and thanked the tree-feller profusely when he returned it in less than half an hour. When she looked out of her window next morning, she discovered that her own ugly monkey-puzzle tree had been lopped at ground level. There were other capers, too numerous to mention, but I shall not forget our trip to the border town of Walkerburn for the seven-a-side rugger finals.

Two Scottish Motor Transport coaches had been hired by the Dick Vet. One was three passengers short. Without invitation cards the students swooped into a staff room and apprehended three professors. Gowns and all they were bundled into the coach and entertained en route from two large hampers; one filled with bottles of Scotch, the other with crusty rolls and hard-boiled eggs. The professors enjoyed it and made no attempt to escape. Rugger songs were sung all the way to the border at great volume and with the right words; from 'The Harlot of Jerusalem' to 'The Ball of Kirriemuir'. After the games were over we all retired to the big barn for dancing, drinking and more singing. Far more than four-and-twenty virgins who had travelled from places other than Inverness had a rattling guid time. Our coach rocked with song on the return trip, but a mouth-organ musician who declined to play a much requested air, 'The Virgin Sturgeon' – because ladies were present – was stripped naked and passed over our heads and placed on the laps of the ladies who had accepted invitations to return with us to Edinburgh. It was a real Scottish rugger day, one which put Llanelli to shame.

I sat my first degree examination in Social Study on Tuesday, 9 December. The subject was Administrative Law. The paper was in two parts and carried seven questions, two to be attempted in Part I, three in Part II. My heart sank when I saw them. I chose the easy ones.

> Give an account of the machinery of public administration in Scotland, describing the places and inter-relation of Central and Local Authorities in the structure.

> Give an account of the powers vested in the Police in Scotland and outline briefly the system of Scottish Police administration.

And if that was not enough to set me back several horse's lengths, I had to endure another ordeal of oral examination, in the same subject, in the Law Retiring Room on 11 December. As I wrote my home address on the envelope provided to send me a pass or failed certificate, I felt I had failed. But I received the best Christmas present of my life on the morning of 15 December. Vera had redirected my envelope to No. 1, Leamington Terrace. It contained the first of my eleven pass certificates. My joy knew no bounds. I telephoned Edwin Muir at Newbattle and read every word to him from that simple, but important piece of paper . . .

PASS CERTIFICATES SHOULD BE PRESERVED — University of Edinburgh, December 1953

SOCIAL STUDY

Cedric W. Mays has PASSED in Administrative Law.
John Orr (Dean)

Edwin and Willa were delighted and asked me to Newbattle for a celebration with malt whisky.

I was inspired by this first result after all my previous frustrations, and pursued my study with increasing energy towards that time on Friday 9 July 1954 when the Graduation Ceremonial was held in McEwan Hall. I would have liked to be present, but I had only nine shillings in the world and had to go to Hayes to work. It would have been a wonderful ending to hear the address to the new graduates from the lips of the Promoter, the gentleman who lectured to me first in the Pollock Hall, Sir Alexander Gray. But I was more than content. From a class of fifty, twelve had passed in Social Study and I had come tenth.

Each of my tutors provided me with a reference to help me find suitable employment. I was convinced that something would turn up after looking at some of the references, two of which had significance, or so I thought.

Department of Organisation of Industry and Commerce
University of Edinburgh
30 June 1954

TO WHOM IT MAY CONCERN

Mr Cedric W. Mays was a student in my class of Organisation of Industry and Commerce during the second half of the academic year 1953–4. He was taking this class as part of his preparation for the University Certificate in Social Study. Among those who were reading Mr Mays secured the first place in my class and a merit certificate, and was consistently conscientious and hard-working and a particularly valuable member of the tutorial groups.

His experience and maturity of judgment are a considerable asset to him and I have no hesitation in recommending him for any post for which his qualification and experience are suitable.

Norman C. Hunt, B.Com., Ph.D., Professor.

The second reference came from my old friend Bill Williams of the Union of Post Office Workers. I felt bound to let him know I had taken his advice, although I was not anticipating standing for Parliament.

HOUSE OF COMMONS

TO WHOM IT MAY CONCERN

During my tenure of office as a General Officer of the Union of Post Office Workers between 1940 and 1952 I came into frequent contact with Mr C. W. Mays, who was for many years the Staff Representative at the Southall Post Office.

Mr Mays exhibited excellent qualities of leadership in those days and I found him a diligent and able local official and a person who could be relied upon to go very fully into the cases which he had to refer to me on behalf of his colleagues. I formed a high opinion of his all-round competency and, in fact, urged him to seek opportunities to further educate himself in social problems. He took my advice and it has given me much personal pleasure to note that despite his lack of early opportunities for study he has done exceedingly well at Newbattle Abbey College and at the University of Edinburgh.

If the position which Mr Mays now seeks has any connection with social welfare I can unhesitatingly support his candidature from the standpoint of ability, integrity and personality.

W. R. Williams
Member of Parliament for Openshaw.

Although I have said many goodbyes in my life, to Auld Reekie – that place where I learned so much of beauty and the good things of this life – I said my goodbye with the greatest regret of all.

Perhaps my ego had become unduly inflated for, like Mr Micawber, I was convinced that something was bound to turn up.